D0217926

# Educational Development

# EDUCATIONAL DEVELOPMENT

Kieran Egan
**FACULTY OF EDUCATION**
**SIMON FRASER UNIVERSITY**

1979
OXFORD UNIVERSITY PRESS
New York

LB
1570
E384

Copyright © 1979 by Oxford University Press, Inc.

Library of Congress Cataloging in Publication Data

Egan, Kieran.
    Educational development.

    Includes index.
    1.  Curriculum change.  I.  Title.
LB1570.E384      375'.001      78-8417
ISBN 0-19-502458-3
ISBN 0-19-502459-1 pbk.

Printed in the United States of America

To
James John and Barbara Wilson Egan
with love

12-82 Gift R. Sylvester

# ACKNOWLEDGMENTS

I would like to thank those colleagues at Simon Fraser University who have read drafts of this book and have made many valuable suggestions for its improvement. It is a pleasure to be able to express here my thanks in particular to Cornel Hamm, Roger Gehlbach, Tasos Kazepides, Sheila O'Connell, and Maurice Gibbons. I benefited considerably from the encouragement and the good advice of David Nyberg of the State University of New York at Buffalo; from the continuing valuable teaching of my Ph.D. Chairman, D. Bob Gowin of Cornell University; and from the useful criticism and suggestions so kindly given by Susan Milmoe of Cambridge University Press. Shona McLean has expertly typed the manuscript and its revisions, offering helpful suggestions in the process, for all of which I am most grateful. Susanna Egan has helped make much of the manuscript more readable and has made so many contributions in discussion that it would be impossible to disentangle what parts are due to her.

*Vancouver, B.C.*
*May 1978*           K. E.

# CONTENTS

# Educational Development

*Fourteen-year-old, why must you giggle and doat,*
*Fourteen-year-old, why are you such a goat?*
*I'm fourteen years old, that is the reason,*
*I giggle and doat in season.*

Stevie Smith, "The Conventionalist"

# INTRODUCTION

In 1959, David P. Ausubel noted that the scientific study of growth and development had made great advances but that it could offer "only a limited number of very crude generalizations and highly tentative suggestions"[1] to the educational practitioner. Since 1959, there has been rapid growth in our knowledge of psychological, moral, social, physical, conceptual, and other kinds of development. Vast amounts of empirical research have probed and tested the various theories advanced, forcing further revisions and refinements, and educators have continued to scrutinize this work for knowledge that is of use to the practical activities of teaching and learning. Today, we may confidently claim that these disciplines still offer the educational practitioner only a limited number of very crude generalizations and highly tentative suggestions.

Why is this? It seems so intuitively obvious that a refined theory and its supporting knowledge about, say, concept development

[1] David P. Ausubel, "Viewpoints from Related Disciplines: Human Growth and Development," *Teachers College Record* 60 (1959): 245–54.

should be directly applicable to education. Why do such theories yield only crude generalizations and vague recommendations of no greater precision than those any teacher with half a grain of common sense can offer? Ausubel claimed it was due to the failure to appreciate the distinction between a pure and an applied science. The disciplines that study development, learning, and motivation aim to discover general laws as ends in themselves. Ausubel pointed out that application of the discoveries of the pure sciences to practical educational situations requires additional research "at the engineering level of operations." Furthermore, according to Ausubel, the intuitive sense that one can go directly from the findings of these pure sciences to education "has caused incalculable harm," and has led to "fallacious and dangerous . . . overgeneralized and unwarranted applications"[2] in educational theory and practice.

The claim that educational applications of theories generated in pure disciplines have been at best vacuous and at worst dangerous represents a powerful challenge to the major industry concerned with communicating these theories and their "implications" to teachers and to education students. The challenge is made even stronger by the plausibility of the claim, especially if the typical introductory psychology of education text is to count as evidence. There we find lengthy sections on Jean Piaget's theory of stages of development, with a brief concluding section labeled something like "Implications for Teaching," which announces that one should not use an exclusively verbal method of presentation to very young children, or that one should not expect the young to understand very abstract concepts. These "insights" hardly come as news to the average teacher.

This is not to depreciate Piaget's work: part of a proper appreciation of his work's value involves not abusing it by trying to extend it in ways that are facile and inappropriate. Piaget has contributed enormously to our understanding of children's intellectual development. The *focus* of his theory, however, is not education but genetic epistemology. The knowledge that generated the

[2] Ibid., p. 246.

theory and the further knowledge and inquiries generated by the theory are determined by the theory's focus. The fact that teachers are interested in certain topics Piaget has studied does not magically convert his theories and knowledge into a form directly applicable to education's practical concerns. At present, it seems that educational research is dominated by psychological theories that lead to knowledge of psychological value and interest but that offer only occasional "implications" for education. An educational theory of learning, development, or motivation should be composed from, and focus back onto, those phenomena of most interest to educators. Such a theory will likely involve a different level of generality and a different range of phenomena from those which interest psychologists, or sociologists, or genetic epistemologists.

I realize these are opaque claims. In education, we are so bemused by imported theories that the demand for a theory that deals with the phenomena of most interest to us leaves us wondering what such a theory would look like. The only attempt I know of to sketch an educational theory of development, apart from Plato's and Rousseau's, is Whitehead's,[3] though that is very much a bare-boned sketch. What makes it an *educational* theory, however, is simply the fact that it deals with a level of phenomena of direct interest and use to educators.

Ausubel claims that before developmental theories can yield fruit for the teacher preparing a physics or social studies class, a further level of research needs to be carried out. Well, maybe. The research carried out so far at this "engineering level" does not encourage us to wait for more with bated breath. The theories the "engineering" research is to draw from are not educational theories; they do not focus on the *complexity* of educational concerns. They encourage, indeed force, the "engineer" to share their specialized focus.

[3] Alfred North Whitehead, "The Rhythms of Education," *The Aims of Education* (New York: The Free Press, 1967), ch. 2. The theory that follows has some general features in common with Whitehead's. I would be happy to acknowledge him as a source of these ideas, except that I had formulated this theory before having my attention drawn to his. Still, the flow of ideas is always hard to trace, and it does seem quite likely that some of what follows comes indirectly from Whitehead.

No. What we need in education is a *different kind* of theory, one which focuses on the *educational* aspects of development, learning, and motivation and which directly yields principles for engaging children in learning, for unit and lesson planning, and for curriculum organizing. It is this kind of theory that this book offers—a new and comprehensive theory of educational development from earliest years to maturity.

A theory, basically, is a thing to think with—an intellectual tool made from distinctions that conform with the phenomena it is about. Its value depends on how well it conforms with the relevant phenomena, how well it helps to make sense of them, and how well it guides practice, observation, and research to refine and revise its categories and distinctions to conform more closely with the phenomena. The theory of educational development presented here distinguishes four main stages of educational development: mythic, romantic, philosophic, and ironic. The theory's value will be judged initially by how adequately these distinctions and the characterizations of the stages conform with the reader's knowledge, observation, and experience of the process of educational development.

I have suggested that empirical research in this area has not generated much knowledge that is useful for constructing a theory of *educational* development; it is useful, however, for delineating the constraints within which such a theory must fit. This theory is not incoherent with any data derived from empirical testing of theories of psychological, conceptual, sociological, or other development. In addition, I will add support to my theory by showing its coherence at various points with other developmental theories—most prominently Piaget's and Erikson's and data generated by them, and I will refer to work in a range of disciplines which seems to me to support particular claims. In many cases, however, a degree of inference, extrapolation, or interpretation is required to connect such theories and data to my *educational* concerns. Frequently the degree of inference, extrapolation, or interpretation would be at least as much as has to be made from common experience and observation. Therefore, occasionally I will refer readers to common observations or to their own experience of the educational process as a means of supporting some claims. The status of this theory in its present form will be discussed in the conclusions.

The characterization of the stages takes up the first four chapters. The main claim I make is that at each stage we make sense of the world and experience in significantly different ways and that these differences require that knowledge be organized differently to be most accessible and educationally effective at each stage. From the defining characteristics of the stages are derived principles for organizing learning and teaching. I give examples of how these principles would affect the organization of curriculum material.

How far to develop examples is always a problem, as they can easily absorb a great deal of space. Their purpose here is simply to clarify how the principles derived from the characteristics of each stage affect the organization of subject matter. Though the examples should enable teachers to apply the principles to any subject matter they teach, this book is not designed as a practical handbook with worked-out lesson and unit plans. There are many books on methods and techniques for teaching, so, for economy's sake, I will rarely make recommendations about such things. I will, however, assume that when I write "ask $Y$" or "do $X$", the reader will not take these suggestions as literal descriptions of method, but will accept that the ordinary process of the teacher's imaginative interpretation will transform the bare suggestions into say, inquiry activities or projects. The examples, then, should be seen as serving a limited clarifying purpose. I use examples from the social studies, both because I am most familiar with this curriculum area and because the examples will be easily accessible to everyone, in a way that mathematics or physics examples would not be.

The first four chapters state the four stages of educational development and their characteristics. The fifth deals with a variety of qualifications and elaborations that are needed to fill out and make more complex the ideal picture of development presented in the first four chapters. The sixth considers each stage as a "sensitive period" for the development of a particular set of capacities and considers the kind of content that is most appropriate for best encouraging that development. Chapter seven relates the stages to curriculum areas other than the social studies, dealing particularly with English/language arts and the sciences. The conclusions consider an array of issues raised by this theory of educational development.

# 1

# THE MYTHIC STAGE

Approximate ages,
4/5 to 9/10 years

## CHARACTERISTICS
### What children know best

It is a truism that in educating young children, we should start from
what they know best and expand outward from that. This notion, so
obvious to us today, is relatively new. When James Boswell asked
Dr. Johnson what children should learn first, Johnson replied:

> there is no matter what children should learn first, any more
> than what leg you shall put into your breeches first. Sir, you
> may stand disputing which is best to put in first, but in the
> meantime your backside is bare. Sir, while you stand considering
> which of two things you should teach your child first, another
> boy has learnt 'em both.[1]

We still tend to stand disputing while our educational backside is
bare, but, these days, we do have some grounds for thinking it is

[1] James Boswell, *London Journal, 1762–1763*, ed. Frederick A. Pottle (New York:
McGraw Hill, 1950), p. 323.

important that children should learn certain things first and that there is a certain sequence in which things should be introduced.

Acceptance of the truism that one should begin from what children know best has led to various forms of the expanding horizons curriculum. Take, for example, the social studies curriculum that is dominant throughout North America and, increasingly, in Great Britain. We may infer at a glance what its designers assume children know best. It begins with units on families, homes, communities, and so on, those things children have daily contact with. Children, it is assumed, will have developed a concept of family, which can be used as the basis for the content of a unit that expands that concept. That is, despite rhetoric about inquiry-based curricula, the implicit question about what children know best is answered *in terms of content.*

Proponents of a child-centered curriculum propose "relevance to the child's needs" as one of the principles to be used in constructing the curriculum. A teacher might use the child's experience of shopping in a supermarket as a starting point for a unit; and this might lead to lessons on such topics as the typical layout of a supermarket, the sources of various products, the means by which the products are brought to the shelves, making change, the structure of neighborhoods, and other kinds of shops. That is, the child's needs are interpreted in terms of specific content to be learned. Even the more radical approach to early education that claims to construct a curriculum out of children's expressed interests seeks and accepts expression of these interests in terms of content. What alternative is there?

Instead of focusing on such content, we might examine those things that most engage children's interest (for example, fairy stories and games) and try to see "through" their content to the main mental categories children seem to use in making sense of them. I will consider stories and games in more detail below, but even a casual view from this perspective suggests that what children know best when they come to school are love, hate, joy, fear, good, and bad. That is, they know best the most profound human emotions and the bases of morality. Children, for instance, have direct access to the wildest flights of fantasy—to princesses, monsters, and witches in bizarre places and once upon a times. Typical fairy stories are built on vivid and dramatic conflicts involving love, hate, joy, fear, good, bad, and so on. Their engaging power derives from their being the purest embodiments of the most basic emotions and moral conflicts.

This simple observation undermines the foundation of the typical expanding horizons curriculum, allowing us to see that children's access to the world need not be, as it were, along lines of content associations moving gradually out from families, homes, communities, and daily experience, or from things judged relevant on grounds of some kind of physical proximity. Far from condemning ourselves to provincial concerns in the early grades, we may provide direct access to anything in the world that can be connected with basic emotions and morality. We will see what effect this may have on the design of lessons, units, and curricula after considering some characteristics of children's thinking.

## Mythic thinking

I call this first stage of educational development mythic because young children's thinking shares important features with the kind of thinking evident in the stories of myth-using people. I will consider four roughly parallel features.

First, a main function of myth is to provide its users with intellectual security. It does this by providing absolute accounts of why things are the way they are and by fixing the meaning of events by relating them to sacred models.[2] All people look for intellectual security amid the changes of life in the world, and young children in western industrial societies seem to establish a first security in a

[2]For some analyses of mythic thinking useful in this context see Bronislaw Malinowski, "Myth in Primitive Psychology," *Magic, Science and Religion and Other Essays* (New York: Doubleday, 1954); Mircea Eliade, *Myth and Reality* (New York: Harper and Row, 1963); Claude Lévi-Strauss, *The Savage Mind* (Chicago: University of Chicago Press, 1966); Claude Lévi-Strauss, *Structural Anthropology* (New York: Basic Books, 1963); and Claude Lévi-Strauss, *The Raw and the Cooked* (New York: Harper and Row, 1969).

manner not dissimilar from that evident in myth stories. They seek absolute accounts of things, and they want precise, fixed meanings. Young children have great difficulty deriving meaning from the ambiguous and complex. For reasons I will discuss later, children need to know how to feel about a thing in order for that thing to be clear and meaningful; they need to establish some personal and affective relationship with what is being learned.

Second, myth stories and children lack what has been generally called a sense of otherness—concepts of historical time, physical regularities, logical relationships, causality, and geographical space. Some analysts of myth suggest one of myth's functions is to obliterate history, to assert that nothing has changed in the world since the sacred beginning, thus providing a kind of eternally valid charter for things as they are. Children's lack of the concepts of otherness, however, may be accounted for simply as a lack of experience and knowledge of change and causality on a historical scale in a geographical arena.

A third feature of mythic thinking is its lack of a clear sense of the world as autonomous and objective. The conception of the world as an impersonal, objective entity is the achievement of a mature rationality. The child's world is full of entities charged with and given meaning by those things the child knows best: love, hate, joy, fear, good, bad. The world is, as it were, absorbed into the child's vivid mental life. Much more than is the case for an adult, children's imaginative life colors and charges their environment with a meaning derived from within. Piaget has expressed this well in the observation that at this age there is "a sort of confusion between the inner and the outer, or a tendency to fix in objects something which is the result of the activity of the thinking subject."[3]

Fourth, myth stories tend to be articulated on binary oppositions. In the case of myth stories, the oppositions may be between important elements in the life of their users: nature/culture, life/death, raw/cooked, honey/ashes. In the mental life of children, important basic oppositions include big/little, love/hate, security/

[3] Jean Piaget, "Children's Philosophies," *Handbook of Child Psychology*, ed. C. Murchison (Worcester, Mass.: Clark University Press, 1931), pp. 377–91.

fear, courage/cowardice, good/bad. Typical fairy stories are built on sets of such binary opposites, and children tend initially to make sense of things in binary terms, using only a couple of concepts at one time. These binary opposites are then elaborated by a process of mediation between the binary poles. For example, the concepts of hot and cold will normally be learned as the first temperature distinctions. These will then be mediated by warm or by quite hot and quite cold. Thereafter, children may learn to mediate between cold and warm, and warm and hot, leading gradually to a set of concepts along the temperature continuum. Attempts to mediate between other binary opposites perceived in their environments lead to more than simple conceptual elaborations along continua of size, speed, temperature. When the same process tries to mediate between humans and animals, we get those dressed and talking bears, dogs, rabbits that play so prominent a part in children's imaginations. Attempts to mediate between life and death give us ghosts and spirits of various kinds—things that are both alive and dead, as things warm are both hot and cold.

This is not to suggest that children at the mythic stage can understand things *only* if they are put in terms of binary opposites. Greater or lesser elaboration between binary opposites will have been achieved depending on the degree of progress they have made through the stage. However, binary opposites are still fundamental to children's thinking at this mythic stage; even though considerable elaboration from the initial binary terms may have been achieved, meaning derives most clearly from the basic binary distinctions. That is, if something is to be most clearly meaningful, it should be built on and elaborated from clear binary opposites.

Claude Lévi-Strauss concludes that myth stories are also built on or elaborated from basic binary opposites perceived in their users' environments.[4] Lévi-Strauss has also argued, drawing on Roman Jacobson's work in phonetics, that the kind of binary thinking I have alluded to is basic to all thought and reflects a basic structure of

---

[4] See Lévi-Strauss, "The Structural Study of Myths," *Structural Anthropology*; Lévi-Strauss, *The Savage Mind*; and Lévi-Strauss, *The Raw and the Cooked*.

the human mind. Whether or not this is the case, it is evident that such binary structures are prominent in young children's thinking.

These four characteristics of young children's thinking, then, are important because they influence profoundly how children can derive meaning from the world, how they learn, and what they can learn. Taken together, these characteristics help to explain the power of stories in the mental life of young children and lead to clear conclusions for teaching, learning, and motivation. The ability of stories to engage children's interest is worth dwelling on a little more, because features that give stories their power can also be used in engaging children's enthusiasm in learning about the world. First, though, we should consider the general *process* whereby the characteristics of children's thinking outlined above are used in their learning. That is, we should characterize in a general way *how* children learn at the mythic stage.

### Projection and absorption: learning, feeling, and meaning

Learning at the mythic stage involves making sense of the unknown world without in terms of the known world within. The things children have available to learn with are those things they know best, love, hate, joy, fear, good, bad. These are the intellectual tools and conceptual categories that children can employ in making sense of the outside world. The process of learning at the mythic stage involves projecting these known things onto the outside world and, as it were, absorbing the world to them.

Initially, the world becomes known in terms of the basic forms and characteristics of children's mental life. It could hardly be otherwise. Learning is a matter of connecting the known categories to the outside world and fitting the things in the world to them. The clearer the connection between categories and things in the world, the more successful will be the learning. As children develop through the mythic stage, knowledge about the world expands the initial set of mental categories. The world provides not only knowledge as such, but the things in the world that the child perceives and experiences become concepts the child thinks *with*; that is, the child uses the world to think with. I will discuss this in more detail at the beginning of the next chapter when considering the move from the mythic to the romantic stage.

The confusion between inner and outer that Piaget observed, which I have described as the result of making sense of the unknown world without in terms appropriate to the child's mental life, is not a confusion restricted to children. It persists in all of us to a greater or lesser degree, though, in at least one dimension, we measure development in terms of the clarity with which we can distinguish between what is true about the world and what we think about the world. This confusion is also a common feature of myth-using people's thinking.[5] It is not, then, simply an error to be overcome; it is a valid way of making sense of the world and of one's place in it. For young children, it is a *necessary* way of making sense of things and of learning.

This is a point I will repeat in different ways for each stage; we must be sensitive to the changing character of children's thinking and learning and must not see any of the stages as confusions or errors. They are stages of development, and the achievement of further development does not come by hurrying children to make sense of things in more sophisticated ways. The first requirement for educational development is that children develop the characteristics of each stage as fully as possible.

Young children's thinking and learning are in important qualitative ways different from adults'. Children's major intellectual tools and categories are not rational and logical but emotional and moral. This is not a casual nor insignificant difference. It means that access to the world must be provided in the terms of emotion and morality, or knowledge will be simply meaningless. It will always be possible to make children store things in memory and repeat them on request, but such knowledge will remain inert and will contribute nothing toward the development of children's understanding of the world or their place in it. True learning at this stage must involve their being able to absorb the world to the categories of their own vivid mental life and to dialectically use the world to expand the intellectual

[5] See Lévi-Strauss, *The Savage Mind.*

categories they have available. The most effective teaching will be that which provides best access to the world, by organizing what is to be known in terms that children can best absorb and use.

Now we need to see how the characteristics of children's thinking that we have considered lead to principles for organizing knowledge in terms that children can best absorb and use. First, though, let us return to stories and see what clues their engaging power offers towards clarifying such principles.

## The necessity of the story form

It is worth noting that analyses of the fairy stories that most power-fully engage children's interest suggest underlying characteristics similar to those outlined above as the basic characteristics of children's thinking.[6] The Grimm-type stories lack realistic concepts of action, place, change, causality; they make little call on the simul-taneous combination of ideas; the number of characters is small and homogeneous; the characters are composed from one or two out-standing characteristics (big and bad, beautiful and industrious, etc.); the characters are differentiated by simple contrasts, or binary opposites (rich or poor, big or little, obedient or disobedient, clever or stupid); meaning is always clear, in the sense that it is always understood who is to be approved of or disapproved of and what one should feel about the events.

The similarities are hardly surprising, though, given the close relationship between fairy stories, folktales, and myth stories. Like myth stories, fairy stories derive their power from being more or less pure reflections or embodiments of those characteristics basic to children's thinking. These are preeminently the terms in which children can make sense of things; they *understand* things put in these terms.

However, we need to ask what is a story? Perhaps the most important feature of a story is that it is the linguistic unit that can

[6] See Karl Bühler, *The Mental Development of the Child*, trans. Oscar Oeser (London: Routledge and Kegan Paul, 1930).

ultimately fix the meaning of the events that compose it. Take, for example, the event, "He shot Tom." By itself the event is not very meaningful; we don't know how or why or where he shot Tom, or who he and Tom are, or, most important, whether to feel glad or sorry that he shot Tom. The only linguistic unit that can finally answer all these questions is the story. The story, as Aristotle[7] pointed out, has a beginning that sets up expectations, a middle that complicates them, and an end that satisfies them. The meaning of an event in history cannot be fixed in any ultimate way because history has not ended—no one can establish finally that it was good or bad that, say, the French Revolution took place. As new things happen, we constantly reassess the meaning of all past events. We especially reassess how we *feel*—whether it was good or bad, whether we are glad or sorry that this or that happened. With a story, however, the meaning of events may be ultimately fixed. Each event has a place in the whole, and we know we have reached the end of a story when we know what to feel about all the events that compose it.

Another way of saying that the most important feature of stories is that they fix meaning is to say that the most important feature of stories is that they come to an end. That is, they don't just stop. The end involves satisfying the expectations set up in the beginning, thus creating a whole, a unit, within which meaning and feeling are bound together and ultimately fixed.[8]

If a necessary condition of best engaging children's interest in and understanding of knowledge is that it be organized into the kind of unit that fixes meaning and coheres with the other characteristics of children's thinking we have noted, then the story form is not something educators can ignore as significant only for fiction. Indeed, it must lie at the heart of all attempts to make the world meaningful to young children.

Before going on to consider how these characteristics common to simple stories and children's thinking yield principles for how to

---

[7] *Poetics.*

[8] See Frank Kermode, *The Sense of an Ending* (Oxford: Oxford University Press, 1966).

organize lessons and units, it is important to observe a basic distinction between stories and the story form. Stories are composed of fictional content. The story form refers to the abstract structure that underlies the content. This form/content distinction is a little unreal, but it serves to emphasize that my concern is not with the *content* of stories, but with the story *form*. That is, I am *not* advocating that we should tell children stories *about* whatever is to be learned; I am advocating something much more radical—that we use the main features of the simple story form to organize whatever is to be learned.

## Games

This brief analysis of some underlying features of the story form and, by extension, children's thinking may seem to be leading somewhere if we have social studies content in mind. It may, however, appear quite opaque if we try to relate it to the physical sciences or mathematics. The connection between the characteristics of children's thinking and these subjects may become a little clearer when we consider that the features we have found underlying stories are also fundamental to children's games.

That is, young children's games have beginnings, middles, and ends. As with stories, they are thus able to reduce and limit reality, providing an arena within which children may feel secure because they know the rules. Within the limits of the game, the meaning of behavior is established clearly and precisely. In the imaginative content of games, binary opposites—fairies and witches, cops and robbers, war and team games—are common. As with fairy stories, the basic concepts of good, bad, fear, security, love, hate are basic to these games.

The importance of play and games in young children's learning is increasingly being recognized. What is not adequately recognized by educators, however, are the changing characteristics of children's games and the features of the games that are most significant for encouraging learning at different stages of children's educational development. This theory may help to make a few useful initial distinctions in the appropriate characteristics for educational games at different stages. As Iona and Peter Opie have observed:

> When generalizing about children's play it is easy to forget that each child's attitude to each game, and his way of playing it, is constantly changing as he himself matures; his preferences moving from the fanciful to the ritualistic, from the ritualistic to the romantic (i.e., the free-ranging games, "Hide and Seek," "Cowboys and Indians"), and from the romantic to the severely competitive.[9]

Even though the value of games is also increasingly recognized for teaching social studies content, I will concentrate, for economy's sake, on describing social studies examples in terms of the story form. I will consider games only briefly in the following three chapters, keeping more detailed discussion of how they can be used to organize teaching for chapter 7. Even though I discuss the principles derived from the characteristics of children's thinking in terms of the story form, I hope readers will translate those principles into the game form where appropriate.

## TEACHING AND LEARNING
## AT THE MYTHIC STAGE

The purpose of this section is to show how typical curriculum content can be embodied in a story form.

When we begin to organize a unit for very young children, our first question should not be, "How do scholars typically organize this?" or "What are its logical characteristics?" or "What are the most interesting bits?" or "What aspects of the content will children

---

[9] Iona and Peter Opie, *Children's Games in Street and Playground* (Oxford: Clarendon Press, 1969), p. 4. For further discussion of games in education and for an excellent bibliography, see Elliott M. Avedon and Brian Sutton-Smith, *The Study of Games* (New York: John Wiley and Sons, 1971), pp. 315–46. See also Brian Sutton-Smith, *The Folkgames of Children* (Austin: University of Texas Press, 1972); and Jean Piaget, *The Moral Judgement of the Child*, trans. Marjorie Gabain (New York: The Free Press, 1965).

have been exposed to?" The first question should be, "What is mythic about this?" (That is, "mythic" in the sense outlined above.) Think about the subject to be presented through the categories used by a young child. What do you see? How does the subject become organized? The answers should be given in terms of the characteristics of children's thinking outlined above; these will yield direct principles for organizing the unit. Let us first consider the characteristics abstractly and then see what happens when we relate them to the examples.

Young children require a story form. They require a beginning that sets up an expectation, a puzzle, a problem, or what writers call a sense of tension. A unit should begin as a story begins; it must engage interest, and that interest must be so central that it can be developed and sustained and resolved at the end but not before the end. Developing a concept or conveying a specific body of knowledge *without* creating such a central expectation that is, in the end, resolved, prevents children from knowing how to feel about the concept or content. A storylike unit, in other words, provides precise affective orientation to the material and conveys it, accordingly, in a way that children understand. A storylike unit will set up expectations, develop them, and finally resolve them.

Young children require binary opposites, so we will look for the two most powerful and basic conflicting forces or elements or concepts or characters in our topic. The beginning, then, will set up an expectation from the dramatic conflict between these binary forces. Because children make sense of the world primarily in terms of those things they know best, the forces should be embodiments of a primary conflict between good/bad, big/little, brave/cowardly.

The conflicting forces should be personified to some degree. Causality, for example, should not be represented in abstract logical terms, but in terms of actions being willed by the major forces. "England was greedy and wanted to become richer, so it conquered people all over the world, took their raw materials and forced them to buy English goods." Whether or not this is accurate, it is the kind of personification that is appropriate to the child's understanding of England's actions. During the mythic stage, children are developing a sense of the distinction between human emotions, human will, and what causes the behavior of physical entities or, in this example, a country. But the distinction does not become sufficiently refined as to require different concepts until the next stage. Indeed, it is the development of this perceived need for a distinct set of concepts that heralds the move to the next stage. That is, young children increasingly realize that countries do not feel and think the same way that they do, but during the mythic stage the concepts they use to understand their own behavior are the only ones they have available to understand that of countries. Using such personifications should present no confusions at this stage; the degree to which children have developed the distinction will be reflected in the degree to which they understand the personified concepts as having a metaphorical meaning.

The main principles we have for organizing our unit derive from: story form; binary oppositions; absolute meaning; lack of concepts of otherness and sense of an autonomous, objective world; emotional and moral categories.

*Example 1.1 The Story of Civilization* What is civilization about in a mythic perspective? We have a range of possible ways of representing it. The basically religious vision of history as a conflict between good and evil is probably the most accessible. Zoroaster's representation of the universe as a dramatic struggle between light and dark has been one of the most powerful and influential ideas in history. We might wisely borrow and secularize it to find our binary conflict. The story of civilization can be presented as the struggle between knowledge and ignorance, which, using Zoroaster's terms in a metaphorical sense, can be visualized as light and darkness. These are hardly unfamiliar terms, being basic to the way so many people in the west have viewed history.

Our beginning must introduce the drama in such a way as to create an expectation, a sense of tension, a puzzle. We may begin, then, with an image of primitive people involved in a daily struggle against hunger, disease, natural disasters, the destructive ambitions of others, wars, and the usual human vices that undermine civilized life. Civilization is the story of people cooperating to defend themselves against these varied threats. The darkness constantly threatens to overwhelm the frail defences of the light. Our unit will look at various civilized groups, some of which were obliterated by the darkness, some of which managed to throw out a spark that caught and lit elsewhere, some of which flickered and glimmered and blazed and spluttered again.

The middle of the unit will involve a variety of smaller stories about specific ways people gathered together and kindled the light of knowledge and tried to defend it. In each case, the struggle to preserve the light of knowledge against external threats, internal vices, institutional ossification will form the focus of attention. Ignorance of soil exhaustion for instance, the sack of Rome, various demonstrations of human greed, fear, hate, anxiety will all be forms of darkness that threaten the light of knowledge and civilization. The love and joy of St. Francis, the energy, courage, and nobility of Pericles, Alfred, and Charlemagne, for instance, will all be sources of light. The unit can end with a consideration of the greater defences civilized light has built against darkness during the nineteenth and twentieth centuries: in enormously expanded knowledge; in a scientifically based technology; and in the liberal and humane institutions of modern societies.[10] We might add that while we are more secure than people have been in the past against hunger, disease, the greed and ambition of others, and so on, our security is still quite frail.

*Example 1.2 North American Indians* Typically in the social studies curriculum in North America, children during their mythic stage learn about the past way of life of one or more Indian tribes. The unit is usually organized around concepts of food, shelter, clothing, artifacts, myths, and these are usually presented as more or less discrete bits that are intended to add up to a culture. The Indians are presented as having lived in a happy inter-

---

[10]I realize that some people might want to object to this kind of value-laden presentation on ideological grounds. My present purpose is to exemplify some principles of content organization; the ideological implications I will discuss later.

action with nature; their social systems functioned smoothly; their clothing and shelters were made and their food gathered from a compliant environment, with which they lived in close harmony; the turn of the year was a leisurely and peaceful swing through a fixed set of activities, punctuated with odd rituals and fun. War is occasionally referred to but never actually takes place. This is no exaggeration. Children are typically presented with a watered down, bowdlerized, anthropological view of a culture.

If a unit about the life of a tribe of Indians begins from a consideration of what is the most profound binary opposition around which knowledge can be organized, we may decide on the conflict between survival and destruction. This is, of course, basic to all cultures and will likely be a quite pervasive theme in early social studies. What does such an organizing principle do to the knowledge it is used to organize?

We will begin our unit by choosing an anecdote or incident that will expose this inherent conflict most powerfully. For example, plains hunters carried enough food for four days; it was the fifth day, and they had not yet found prey. How did they survive? Did they survive? What happened to their families? One can make a small dramatic story of this. Instead of treating the various aspects of their lives as more or less discrete "concepts," each aspect should be seen in terms of the same conflict, exemplifying, elaborating, and vivifying further the constant struggle for survival. Shelters, for example, would not be seen only in terms of their structure and appropriateness, but would be considered primarily as machines built against the destructive threats of nature. This would draw attention to the limits of their ability to protect. By considering each aspect of the tribe's life in terms of the same basic conflict, one builds a systematic image of the culture as first a defence against nature's destructiveness and as second an accommodation with nature in its beneficient moods. Presenting nature as having a will and moods is quite appropriate during the mythic stage. The presentation makes nature comprehensible in a way that an ironic "witless nature" cannot be comprehensible to children, and the terms of this pathetic fallacy, even if understood more or less literally, will by gradual degrees be understood metaphorically as the child develops.

From a unit on Indians that is organized on the binary opposition of survival/destruction, children learn that Indians' lives were relatively insecure, that they were open to casual destruction when nature was less than benign, that they were disrupted generation after generation by famine, sickness, inter-tribal war, that their tenuous security was held by often exhausting and brutal labor, and so on. That is, they suffered the lot of nearly all humans, nearly everywhere, through nearly all time. And in what way is this presentation more educationally valuable than the one I have described as typical?

First, and incidentally, one does not have to be a right-wing fanatic to observe the social and individual destructiveness that follows from the tyranny of provincial knowledge and experience over so many modern western children's minds, particularly with regard to their assumption about the easy security of human life and society. They do not normally come to realize that this relative security is very rare and is one of the great achievements of western technological culture; an achievement which only those who have known and can imagine nothing else tend to undervalue. Seeing cultures as systematic defences against destruction and deprivation, rather than as collocations of shelters, clothes, food should tend to encourage respect for their own security and should help them not take it entirely for granted.

Second, this kind of presentation is more educationally valuable for the simple reason that it is more meaningful to children. The typical presentation of a unit on Indians gives the child scraps of information without any clear access to that information or without any way to use it as an "aliment," to borrow Piaget's term, for further educational development. The typical presentation will not, of course, be an absolute waste of time. Children will learn something about a different time and place and style of living. Without recapitulating the reasons given above for the kind of presentation I recommend being more meaningful, it may be stressed here that the conflict between survival and destruction is already

profoundly meaningful to the child. Children know in their very
nervous system what this conflict means—we may elaborate and
become more self-consciously aware of its meaning as we develop,
but when children come to school they have those categories already
available and ready for use. Access to knowledge about Indians' lives
is thus provided by means of the basic terms in which that knowledge is organized.

It will be necessary to organize individual lessons within units like
these on exactly the same principles. Here we might wisely learn
from the soap operas. Within the structure of an overarching story,
they tell a series of mini-stories, each one of which carries forward
the main story, increasing its tension. However, each mini-story has
its own beginning, expectation, middle, and end. Each lesson should
be planned not only to carry on the main story of the unit, but also to
create similar expectations that are elaborated and resolved in the
course of the lesson. Or it may be better to keep the end until the
next lesson, leaving the children cliff-hanging. In the unit on civilization, a lesson might consider the growth of knowledge and light
in threatening circumstances, chart its brightening and something
of its specific character, and elaborate on the darkness threatening it.
One may save the end until the next lesson: "did Roman light
survive or was it overwhelmed?" Then one may begin another
segment with the discovery that some tiny sparks seemed to have
caught tenuously on the far coasts of Ireland and Scotland, but they
were threatened by Vikings and all the usual horrors. "What has St.
Columba got to do with us?" In a story like this, one does not
question his relevance.

It may seem distasteful that educators should learn from fairy
stories and television soap operas, but our concern is meaning and
access to meaning. These ancient and modern forms of popular
entertainment work at or near a mythic level, and we might wisely
examine their power of engaging that immature kind of thinking.
Our purpose is to connect the child's imaginative and vivid feeling
and thinking to the wonders of the real world and to provide the
child with a means of using knowledge about the real world both to

satisfy the psychological needs that fairy stories satisfy and to begin the process of developing a more sophisticated and mature manner of thinking.

From the examples, it may seem that the story form operates only with quite elaborate content over a relatively long period of instructional time. This need not be the case. The story form and its power of engaging interest can be used to communicate content that requires only a few seconds. The U.S. Children's Television Workshop's show *Sesame Street* constantly exemplifies this use of the story form in teaching almost anything, from recognition of the letters of the alphabet to appreciation of the social values of sympathy and kindness.

## CONCLUSION

By allowing *educational* concerns to determine our search, we have reached a more or less unfamiliar characterization of young children's thinking and a quite different way of considering teaching and learning. Successful learning becomes a process of projecting what young children know best onto the world and absorbing the world to their basically emotional and moral conceptual categories. Successful teaching requires being sensitive to these main characteristics of children's thinking and organizing knowledge into a story form so that it may be most readily accessible to them. One of the most important tools for teaching young people becomes a repertoire of story plots and a facility for embodying in them the knowledge to be learned.

I have been primarily concerned in this chapter with what characteristics of young children's thinking tell us about *how* to organize knowledge so that it is most engaging and meaningful. These characteristics also clearly yield principles for selecting *what* content is most appropriate for encouraging children's educational development, and I will consider the matter of appropriate content in some detail in chapter 6.

The mythic stage may be described in general as the critical period for connecting the child's mental life in a meaningful way with the real world. (In chapter 6, I will consider the sensitive or critical period which each stage represents.) An aspect of connecting children's vivid mental life to knowledge about the world, we call the development of imagination; that is, being able to project mental images onto the world and absorb the world to them with ease and flexibility. This connecting process should not serve to restrict and dull the child's mental life. Rather, knowledge about the world should feed it, encouraging G. K. Chesterton's childlike image of a world more full of wonder than we can understand.

The move from the assumptions underlying an expanding horizons structure and those underlying this scheme is not very great. Both schemes accept that one should start from what children know best and build on what they will have learned from family and community life. The crucial difference, as we have seen, lies in identifying what children know best from their earliest years (i.e., their experience of family and community) in terms of emotion and morality, not content. Interpreting relevance to the child's needs in terms of content leads to a curriculum of local and provincial matters. Interpreting relevance to the child's needs in terms of emotions, morality, and the characteristics of thinking identified in this chapter leads to a curriculum of the most dramatic and powerful themes of human life, history, and the natural world. Children have the means of direct access to these; it is our responsibility as educators to facilitate that access in every way our imaginations can suggest.

# 2

# THE ROMANTIC STAGE

## Approximate ages, 8/9 to 14/15 years

### CHARACTERISTICS

From mythic to romantic

The move from the mythic to the romantic stage may be seen in the development of rudimentary but serviceable concepts of "otherness"; concepts of historical time, geographical space, physical regularities, logical relationships, and causality. In developing through the mythic stage, children seem to perceive increasingly clearly that the fundamental emotional and moral concepts derived from a knowledge of self, family, and basic human relationships are inadequate to make full sense of the outside world that they are learning about. Knowledge and experience of the world provide the concepts of otherness. It is in this sense that children begin to use the world to think with.[1] Chairs and countries are increasingly clearly seen to be

---

[1] Or as Piaget writes, "all mental life . . . tends progressively to assimilate the surrounding environment." Jean Piaget, *Six Psychological Studies,* ed. David Elkind and trans. Anita Tenger (New York: Random House, Vintage Books, 1968), p. 8.

inadequately conceived of as thinking, willing, and feeling entities, and they begin to generate in the child concepts appropriate to their particular forms of being and behavior. Another way of putting this is to say that the passage from the mythic stage coincides with the perception that the world is autonomous, is separate, and fundamentally different from the child.

Increasing perception of the primary emotional and moral concepts as inadequate seems to develop gradually through the mythic stage and provides a criterion for measuring progress through that stage. Actual use of the new concepts of otherness, however, seems to happen relatively suddenly. I want to stress that these stages are not simply artificial segmentations in a gradual continuum. They are, of course, to some degree artificial, but they do seem to reflect relatively sudden transitional periods that bring quite fundamental changes to the general character of the way we make sense of things.

With the development from the mythic to the romantic stage, the outside world is no longer securely known as an extension of the inside self, but it is full of strange entities, working by alien laws, unfeeling, vast, mysterious, and threatening. With the development of a sense of an autonomous world comes the reciprocal perception of a self separate from it. During the mythic stage the young child's absorption of the world obviates the need for the child to develop a sense of its separate identity. "Le monde, c'est moi!" the young child assumed. Children face two immediate and connected tasks in order to establish a sense of intellectual security in the romantic stage: first, they must forge a new relationship and connections with the autonomous world and so achieve some method of dealing with its threatening alienness, and, second, they have to develop a sense of their distinct identity.[2] I will mark the move from the mythic to the romantic stage by using the term *student* rather than *child*.

---

[2] It will be evident that this reflects in large part Erikson's fifth developmental task, the integration of ego identity in face of the threat of role confusion though, of course, in a different context and with regard to largely different phenomena from those I go on to discuss. See Erik H. Erikson, *Childhood and Society*, 2d ed. (New York: W. W. Norton, 1963), pp. 261–63.

## Romantic associations

The most apparent response students make to the threat posed by the newly perceived alien world is to associate themselves with those elements in the world that are most powerful, noble, courageous; in short, with those things that preeminently transcend the threats the world poses to the immature ego.

An association with the ingenuity and courage of Ulysses or Captain Kirk of the Starship Enterprise, or with the nobility and determination of Florence Nightingale or St. Teresa of Avila, involves the student's ego in the implicit claim that "I could do that too," or, rather, "I *am* doing that too." Students, then, no longer need to fear the vast mysterious world that is opening up before them because they can transcend every threat by means of romantic associations. By such means the threats are transmuted into adventure.

This capacity to associate oneself with powerful forces, characters, movements, ideas seems to be a development of the mythic capacity to connect with the world by means of those best known emotions and bases of morality. Just as the child at the mythic stage can absorb any information provided in these familiar terms, the student at the romantic stage may form associations with anything in the universe embodying those qualities that best transcend the challenges posed by daily living in the real world: qualities like courage, nobility, fortitude, genius, power, energy, creativity, and so on. Again, we see that children have a means of direct access to almost anything in the universe, and need not be led outwards, as it were, along content associations. Indeed, it will be argued below that children most naturally explore the real world completely the other way about; they begin at the outside limits and work in.

The connected tasks of establishing a sense of intellectual security and a sense of identity in an alien world are successfully achieved by romantic association with the most powerful and transcendent things the student learns about.[3] Such a process, of course,

---

[3] In chapter 5, I will discuss what happens when the move from stage to stage is either not achieved at all or is achieved with only partial success. In chapters 1-4, I am outlining an ideal educational development.

supports and glorifies the ego. Romantic students essentially deify themselves, and this is *necessary* for the establishment of a first security within a world of alien reality. It is not a fault or vice that needs to be eradicated as quickly as possible. It needs to be fed with knowledge of the powerful and transcendent in every discipline, both to help students develop through this stage and to help them feel in themselves the power and glory of the real world. Their glorified identities derive from identifying with the glorious.

## Romantic reality

At the mythic stage, the major categories the child uses to think with determine how the world is perceived to work. At the romantic stage, the student's mind has to accommodate itself to the alien rules of how the world in fact works. That is to say, students have to develop their romantic sense of identity within a context of *reality*. The typical romantic manner of exploring and discovering what is real and possible in the world seems to involve a development of the mythic thinker's use of binary opposites. Instead of projecting binary opposites from within, however, the romantic mind searches outside itself to the *limits* of the world for external binary opposites within which reality exists.

A defining characteristic of the move into the romantic stage, then, is the development of a quite sudden fascination with the extremes of what exists and what is known. In the mythic stage, the sense of scale pays no heed to the limits imposed by reality; for example, going toward the king's throne, the hero may have to pass a series of guards, the biggest of which is three miles high and the smallest of which is no larger than your thumb nail. At the romantic stage, students' interest in scale similarly focuses on the extremes, but is constrained by reality. Thus, *The Guinness Book of World Records* fascinates the romantic student with its accounts of the biggest, the smallest, the fastest, the highest, the furthest, and so on. It is between such extremes that students locate reality and within them that they construct their identity.

I call this stage romantic because it shares with romanticism the tension that comes from the desire to transcend a threatening reality while seeking to secure one's identity within it. The mythic projection that treated reality with contempt now has to be, reluctantly, confined within it. So romance is, as it were, myth confined to the real world, but it constantly beats against its limits.

An important characteristic of knowledge that engages students at the romantic stage is that it tells them something about what is real and possible. The impossible fantasies of the mythic stage are quite suddenly treated with contempt as "stupid kids' stuff." A further characteristic required for knowledge to be engaging at this stage is that it be *different*; different from everything mundane and conventional, different from everything the students have known and experienced. Just as romantic exploration of the real world begins with the probing of its limits, so it is the fantastic and spectacular that the romantic perception highlights. Erich Von Daniken and Immanuel Velikovsky are more interesting guides to history than Arnold Toynbee or Karl Marx; Herodotus, his text packed with wonders and Guinness-Book-of-Ancient-Records details, is more interesting than Thucydides.

To use an analogy: the mythic stage might be seen as a cognitive recapitulation of Sigmund Freud's primary process. As the baby does not distinguish the world from itself, so the young child has no separate concepts to distinguish the world's working from that of its own mind. Similarly, the romantic stage may be seen as a cognitive recapitulation of Freud's secondary process. As the ego dominates the personality and demands gratification from everything, so the romantic mind is interested in the world only to the degree that it satisfies the desire for difference, for the spectacular, the fantastic, the extreme, and, thus, to the degree that it gives pleasure.

This romantic search for limits enables students to explore the vastness of the worlds of nature, culture, and history, to get a sense of their size and scope, and to get a sense of what is real within them. This is, as it were, the period of sniffing around and establishing boundaries; only when boundaries are securely known does one turn and explore the world within them.

As with the mythic stage, few content restrictions affect what can be taught successfully during the romantic stage. Anything with which a romantic student can associate, anything that involves the characteristics outlined above, becomes "relevant to students' needs." One needs simply to be sensitive to these characteristics and to organize the material at hand accordingly. I will demonstrate below the organization of material that best engages interest and promotes understanding for this stage.

One reflection of students' desire to explore limits and to form personal associations with whatever is to be learned leads students to want to know "What was it like then, or there, or doing that?" They want to sense different forms of human life but not in the way that a scholar might. Their concern is to *feel* different forms of life, to try them on, as it were. Realistic detail becomes important; and the more different from the student's experience, the better. Incas and an imaginary martian colony have a head start over the histories and lives of their grandparents. The association is made personal *not* through proximity of relationship or physical familiarity but through those human qualities that lead to a transcendence over the everyday and commonplace world. Grandparents' lives can, of course, be made engaging by these principles, but, in general, it seems to me much easier to engage teenage students at a romantic stage with a medieval scholar/saint like Ramon Lull than with knowledge about grandparents' lives. It is not the development of the students' own society that will be most engaging, but that of the most exotic and bizarre societies. Having established a sense of the limits of possible societies, they will have a framework to begin making sense of their own. Before developing such a framework, details of their own society will remain largely meaningless in any educational sense.

### Romantic stories

We might again get some clues about how best to organize knowledge so that it engages students at this stage by looking briefly at the kinds of stories that most appeal to them. I am clearly not using *romantic stories* to mean only the kind of love stories to which the term commonly refers. Here, a romantic story is one in which a hero or heroine (or institution, nation, idea), with whom or with which the reader may identify, struggles against odds to a glory and transcendence over threatening nature (or persons, events, institutions, ideas, nations), in which glory the reader may then share. Such stories have a crucial characteristic that makes them ideal for this stage—they are ego-supporting. They allow and encourage the reader to associate with some noble and powerful force that achieves success against a threatening world. Occasionally, they allow the hero or heroine to die or lose, but only in a context which enables the reader to deliciously share the hero's or heroine's moral or other superiority, which is not recognized by the unfeeling world.

Karl Bühler calls the stories that most appeal at this stage the "Hans Christian Anderson-type." They have more complex plots than the Grimm-type. They are realistic. Even when they deal with imaginary worlds, there is always a concern with realistic detail or plausibility. They have clear and powerful heroes and heroines. They tend to have exotic, though realistic or plausible, settings. They are often concerned with the differences between people who have more complex motives than those in the Grimm-type stories. Their meaning is always clear, in the sense that readers know clearly what they should feel about the events and characters. Bühler mentions *Robinson Crusoe* as a paradigm of this kind of story—one might add much of science fiction, adventure stories, animal stories to this category.

Again, we are considering what characteristics of stories appeal at this stage not in order to select stories for students but to learn about the character of students' thinking, about the kinds of meaning they seek, and, consequently, about how we should organize knowledge so that it is most accessible, meaningful, and engaging to students at this stage.

Similar changes may be seen in the kinds of games that appeal to children at this stage. Again, *reality* plays a centrally important role. Games that do not adhere to a realistic or plausible world are rejected contemptuously as "kid's games." Romantic games involve a hesitant, ambivalent grappling with serious problems in a context insulated by playfulness. Intellectual games become important, particularly those that serve the general search for the limits of what is possible and for the necessarily true. Zeno's paradoxes, for example, tend to become fascinating, as does the kind of playful dealing with serious ideas found in Lewis Carroll.

## Detail

A further aspect of students' search for limits during the romantic stage is evident in the development of obsessive hobbies and pastimes. There is a desire to learn something exhaustively or collect something completely: to know the score of every football game played by the team with which an association is formed; to collect every postage stamp of a particular era and place; to know every detail of the life and to collect every photograph of a film star or member of royalty; to know the shape of every leaf of every tree; to know everything about Saturn or about costume through the ages. It is a kind of intense specialization, but I think it is more properly seen as a further expression of the desire to find the limits of things. By exhaustively knowing something, one gets a sense of the scale of everything.

The obsession with detail may be seen in the science fiction films or television series that most interest students at a romantic stage. There is virtually no positive correlation between the quality or even good sense of the stories and the amount of interest generated. There is a very high correlation between interest generated and the amount of money spent in creating precise realistic, Robinson Crusoe-like detail.[4] Students' interest and their educational development through this stage will be fed by the opportunity to spend time learning some part of any unit in massive detail. A unit on the medieval world, for example, might provide an opportunity for

[4] In 1977, the film *Star Wars* proved to be one of the most popular films ever made. Some of the principles outlined so far help to explain its success. It is articulated on a simple mythic conflict of good versus bad, and it appeals to the romantic fascination both with a power that allows the hero to transcend mundane reality and with awe-inspiring detailed illusions of *different* worlds and images.

some students to look at David Macaulay's wonderfully romantic book, *Cathedral*.[5] This is an account of the building of a fictional medieval cathedral, or rather of a typical composite cathedral. There is just sufficient text to provide a story context for the beautifully detailed drawings of each stage in the building. The impact of the page by page gradual rise of the enormous structure in the middle of the crowded, walled town is fantastic. Many students at a romantic stage go from the book to ransack libraries for yet more and more knowledge about the building of cathedrals, about medieval towns, about the medieval church, and so on.

With this zest for collecting or exhausting an area of knowledge comes an ability to memorize and retain massive amounts of detail, with an efficiency apparently much superior to any other stage of one's life. The educational significance of this characteristic is obvious. The problem, however, is to harness it to the mastery of the kind of material that will best help the student's educational development. The way to do this will be discussed in the following section.

### Sentimental education

This book begins with a verse from Stevie Smith about the giggling and doating of a fourteen year old. Giggling and doating are aspects of the sentimentality that is a prominent part of the romantic stage. Sentimentality is sentiment out of control, sentiment that is excessive or inappropriate to its chosen object. Excesses of love, devotion, hatred, rejection are common in romantic students. The excess is occasionally seen in immoderate reserve or withdrawal, a fear of expressing any sentiment at all.

The development of sentiment is not a gradual and orderly step by step process. It seems to begin suddenly and wildly, with students' sentiments flooding uncontrolled all over the place, and then, ideally, is brought gradually to proportionate expression for ap-

[5] David Macaulay, *Cathedral: The Story of Its Construction* (Boston: Houghton Mifflin, 1973). See also his other books: *City: A Story of Roman Planning and Construction* (Boston: Houghton Mifflin, 1974); *Pyramid* (Boston: Houghton Mifflin, 1975); *Underground* (Boston: Houghton Mifflin, 1976); and *Castle* (Boston: Houghton Mifflin, 1977).

propriate objects. The process is one of excess and extremes being gradually controlled. It is, again, a kind of exploration of limits and extremes, locating appropriate and proportionate sentimental attachments within these.

Sentimentality, which is so embarrassing to many people, is not inappropriate at the romantic stage. If learning how to proportionately allot sentiment to appropriate objects comes by gradual control and refinement from initially uncontrolled sentimental excesses, then to suppress the excesses is to undermine the possibility of the student learning to control them.

Sentimental immaturity seems quite common in our culture, and this is reflected in our teachers. Immature adults often defend with cynicism and ridicule their inability to handle students' sentimentality. Romantic students should not be made to feel shame about expressions of sentiment that are disproportionate to their objects. They should be encouraged and helped sympathetically toward increasing control.

Romantic students defend themselves against the inner wildness and lack of control of their sentiments by extreme outward conformity. During the romantic stage students are greater conventionalists than at any other period of their lives. The rigidity of their conformity to styles and fashions of clothes and of hair is proportionate to their inner lack of control. The fear that accompanies this lack of control is evident also in the ridicule addressed to those who do not conform.[6]

## TEACHING AND LEARNING
## AT THE ROMANTIC STAGE

The first question we ask about the material to be taught at this stage is, "What is romantic about this?" and the answer will be

[6] I have suggested that this conformity is in part a defensive response to typical adolescent students' initial difficulties in controlling sentiments. This, in turn, I would locate as a part of what Erikson has called more generally their "identity confusion"—conformity to a group's mores and fashions being a defense against this. See Erik H. Erikson, *Childhood and Society*, 2d ed. (New York: W. W. Norton, 1963), p. 262.

given in terms of the characteristics outlined above. That is, our romantic organization will involve an exploration of reality in detail, concepts of otherness, access through something as different as possible from students' everyday experience, and connection to the different element by means of association with some transcendent human quality.

In addition, because students still require determinate meaning in order fully to make sense of what is being learned, the story form is important. Students at the romantic stage do not require the absolute meaning of the mythic stage, so the story form may be somewhat more diffuse and more sophisticated than before. But, they do require sharper beginnings and endings to units than a mature adult understanding would normally consider proper. Opposing elements in dramatic conflict, therefore, and setting up and resolving an expectation, will still be important features, but we no longer need the stark primitive polar opposites of the mythic stage.

Below, I will show how these principles can be used in organizing a unit on the Industrial Revolution. Following that I will consider a unit that more readily lends itself to a romantic presentation: a unit on ancient Greece. The desirability of introducing students to this Graeco-Roman period will be discussed in chapter 6.

*Example 2.1 The Industrial Revolution* What comes into focus when we view the Industrial Revolution from a romantic perspective? (Romantic is used here only in terms of the characteristics outlined above, not in any other sense.) How do we best provide students at the romantic stage with access to the meaning of the revolution? The typical response of those who work with the expanding horizons assumptions is to look for aspects of the Industrial Revolution with which students are already familiar. Typically, they begin with children and consider that many of them had to work long and brutal hours in coal mines and in factories. This does, of course, have an immediate romantic appeal, but it is quickly exhausted and does not lead easily to a sense of what the Industrial Revolution was primarily about.

Drawing on the principles outlined above, we will look not for something with which students will be familiar but for something that will be entirely strange. We will look for something far from anything they will have experienced but which nevertheless can be connected to them by some transcendent quality with which they can associate. Furthermore, this quality should also lead them to the heart of the Industrial Revolution.

One might begin by showing the students a picture of Isambard Kingdom Brunel. There were a few photographs taken of Brunel in 1857, one of which is available in Great Britain and North America as a poster. The name alone is odd. In the photographs, he appears a small, stiff, top-hatted Victorian in a crumpled black suit and dusty boots. He seems a million miles from anything modern students have access to. We have, then, our something different; how do we connect students with him and, through him, with the Industrial Revolution?

One may talk about Brunel for a minute or so, telling the students just a few basic facts about him. In the background of the photograph mentioned above are the iron chains specially forged to launch his ship the *Great Eastern*. The technology for building iron ships had only recently been mastered, and the biggest so far had been 700 tons. Brunel's *Great Eastern* was 22,500 tons. It was large enough to make trans-Atlantic travel positively comfortable. Brunel also built the Great Western Railway across the south and west of England, leveling hills, bridging valleys with some of the most beautiful and ingeniously designed iron bridges ever built, and driving tunnels through miles of solid rock. He was most fascinated by what was supposed to be impossible, and all his plans and designs bordered on the limits of the possible—some failing, others triumphing. When he was only twenty, he built the first tunnel under the Thames, to be used for the underground railway. Half way through, he cleared everything up, brought in banqueting tables and chandeliers, and gave a huge banquet for London's dignitaries. Typical of him, further along the tunnel, he gave an equally splendid banquet for one hundred and fifty of his laborers.

Students, then, may be connected with the odd little Victorian in the hazy photograph by means of his confidence, power, courage, energy, daring, ingenuity.

These qualities, with which the student wants to associate, are also the means by which the student may move from Brunel to an understanding of the Industrial Revolution itself. As students have access to Brunel through his confidence, courage, and energy, so, too, they can have access to the Industrial Revolution as an expression of these same qualities.

The interest generated by connecting students with something far from their experience needs to be sustained and developed. It must lead toward as fully meaningful an understanding of the Industrial Revolution as possible. The technical tool that will help us achieve so much is the story form. We still need to generate a binary conflict which will develop an expectation, a sense of tension that can be satisfied by the ending of the unit. Already we have identified the protagonist in our drama as the energy and confidence embodied initially in Brunel. A conflicting force may be seen in fear; fear of crop failure, fear of change and the unknown, fear of speed, fear of foul weather at sea, fear of all the things that make life nasty, brutal, and short. The story unit on the Industrial Revolution may be presented as a confrontation between confidence and energy on the one hand and fear of change and the unknown on the other.

It will, of course, be necessary to present students with William Blake's or John Ruskin's vision of the Industrial Revolution as a creator of filth and horror and as the brutalizer of men, women and children in degrading labor. But the roar of Blake's dark, satanic mills must also be heard as a roaring expression of human energy. Certainly it was a period that shows starkly the exploitation of human by human, but that is not all the Industrial Revolution was about. Look out any window and you see its triumphs as well as its scars, and, if you look at its heroic intellectual as well as material products, you cannot but feel the fascinating adventure into which its amazing burst of confident energy has flung this planet. It is this that grips the student's imagination at the romantic stage, and it is association with this confident energy that helps the student establish a secure identity in the world created by the Industrial Revolution. Only by these means will students develop through this educational stage to more sophisticated perceptions both of themselves and of the specific material they have mastered.

The middle of our romantic unit will sustain the expectation set up by seeing the Industrial Revolution as a conflict between confident energy and fear. Our focus then will be on those things that best exemplify the two qualities and show them in conflict. Examples of confident energy will include the key inventions that made the revolution possible. These must not, however, be presented only as a series of technical achievements. Rather, they should be thought of in terms of the quality with which we want students to associate, and this is usually best achieved by presenting the inventions as products of the lives and personalities of their inventors; that is, as expressions of their confident energy. The other force that sustains our story should not be forgotten; the inventions and the changes they create should continually be counterpointed by the problems they raise. We will stress here those very varied elements that complicate the unbridled expression of this confident energy: technical failures; the damage and destruction of beautiful country and harmonious life styles; the ruthlessness (see Blake's and Ruskin's diatribes); the aristocratic contempt for new manufacturing wealth as against wealth derived from land; attempts at political controls over labor conditions. Elaboration of our story at this stage adds sophistication; the confident energy may be seen to tend toward excess, toward ruthless manipulation. The student's association should not be destroyed by this, but only refined; that is, their romantic association will be with those good expressions of confident energy and, though they recognize the quality can also yield bad expressions, they will restrict their association so as to exclude these.

The end requires some kind of resolution. What happened in the clash of confident energy and fear? A sophisticated understanding might want to argue that the outcome is still unclear, that this opposition is no longer a good way to view the processes set in motion by the Industrial Revolution. Students at this stage, however, need some sense of closure, some conclusion that clarifies what they should feel about all the elements that have constituted the beginning and middle. The end, on the other hand, need not be an absolute assertion.

We may end our unit with a generalized picture of the world as changed by the Industrial Revolution. It created a kind of world undreamed of both by those who created the revolution and by those who opposed it. It is neither the utopia preached by some nor the nightmare predicted by others. A conclusion might well be a multimedia presentation of the best things that have resulted from the confident energy that created the Industrial Revolution; speed, powerful engines, machines, roads, bridges, huge cities, massive buildings, images of increased health, wealth, and freedom, and so on.

Clearly, these are not the only terms in which one may view the Industrial Revolution. My concern here is not to make claims about the revolution, but simply to show how the principles derived from the characteristics of students' thinking at this stage can be applied to organizing any topic. The same principles could lead to a multitude of different approaches; the Blakean vision of ordered harmony might be presented as the characteristic with which students could associate, and the opposition could be wild, improvident technological innovation. Or wholly different qualities could form the basic structuring opposition. To try to present an adult's perception, however, by adding qualifications and complexities—by stressing, for example, the excesses to which confident energy may lead—is simply to deprive students of access to the material.

*Example 2.2 The Glory that was Greece* Herodotus' *Histories* is one of the best guides for presenting the history of ancient Greece in a romantic way. The book by itself, of course, is largely inaccessible to typical modern students, but Herodotus seems to exemplify most of the characteristics of the romantic stage; his book is full of fascinating details, is concerned with the extreme achievements of the hitherto largely unknown world of the East, is articulated on a binary opposition between Greek liberty and Persian tyranny, and is organized in a story form that sets up the opposition early, develops it in a diffuse middle, and concludes it in the defeat of the huge tyrannous Persia by small, courageous, and liberty-loving Greece.

To begin, then, we might borrow Herodotus' opposition between liberty and tyranny. We need also something different, something that will take us to the heart of the quality of the Greek sense of liberty with which we want students to associate. One could begin with Herodotus' story of Croesus. The phenomenally wealthy Persian king asks the wise Athenian, Solon, "Who is the happiest man you have ever seen?" Herodotus tells us:

> The point of the question was that Croesus supposed himself to be the happiest of men. Solon, however, refused to flatter, and answered in strict accordance with his view of the truth. "An Athenian," he said, "called Tellus."
>
> Croesus was taken aback. "And what," he asked sharply, "is your reason for this choice?"
>
> "There are two good reasons," said Solon, "first, his city was prosperous, and he had fine sons, and lived to see children born to each of them, and all these children surviving; and, secondly, after a life which by our standards was a good one, he had a glorious death."[7]

Croesus then asks who is the second happiest, but again was told about Greeks whose lives embodied those virtues and good fortune the Greeks prized most highly—the virtues of free men living harmonious lives.

Greek history is full of incidents that could be used to engage interest in something different that directly carries one to the center of our unit's opposition. One might role-play Aristeides the Just

---

[7] Herodotus *Histories* I. 31 (trans. Aubrey de Sélincourt, Harmonsworth: Penguin Books, 1954), pp. 23–24.

being approached by a blind beggar. Aristeides was an Athenian leader, honored and respected, a moderate and wise man. The beggar, not knowing who he is, asks him to mark the name *Aristeides* on a piece of pottery and put it into the jar in which votes were put for exile. "Why," Aristeides asks the beggar, "do you want Aristeides to be exiled?" "Because I can't bear hearing anyone called 'the Just.'" Needless to say, Aristeides helps the blind beggar. The role-play can involve others in creating the context and meaning of the incident, showing how the Athenians would send into exile even the best and most prominent citizens simply because they were becoming too respected and too influential. Such power would likely lead to pride, and pride would upset a person's sense of harmony and justice. The liberty of all, including the exiled, would best be preserved by the maintenance of harmony.

If either of these incidents is our beginning, we need to see this Greek harmony and liberty in contrast to, and then in conflict with, Persian luxury and tyranny. Our middle might follow Herodotus around the eastern and southern lands conquered by the Persians (Persian meaning "destroyer"), characterizing them by means of Herodotus' most choice and vivid stories and details. The tension may be increased by a discussion of the constant clashes between the tiny Greek states and the massive Persian Empire and the sense that soon the all-devouring tyrannous Persians would turn on and devour the Greeks as well. This will lead to the enormous armies collected by Persia to crush the Greeks and the amazing battles at Marathon, Thermopylae, and Salamis, with all their dramatic force and fascinating detail.

The unit might end with the Greek success and the rise of the Athenian Empire. One might conclude it with a consideration of the wonders created by the outburst of the Greek spirit of liberty. After such a unit, most students would be moved by Pericles' Funeral Oration read directly from a clear translation of Thucydides. Such an ending has in it the germ of an expectation that could begin a second unit on ancient Greece. Here the conflict might be between order and strife, involving the tragedy of Athens' fall, the endless bloodshed of inter-city war, and ending in the career of Alexander, the ideal romantic hero who blazed across the world like fire from heaven.

One of the dangers at this stage, under pressure of students' ready withdrawal to boredom, is that of being driven to pick out all the romantic bits and string them more or less loosely together. It is not just the bits that need to be romantic, however, to sustain interest; the bits have to be felt as coherent parts of a romantic whole. That is, the *unit* must be organized romantically. This can be problematic, in that students at this stage do require constant romantic bits to sustain interest. Again, one may consider the typical soap-opera format of stories within a story. History is best understood at this stage as a kind of mosaic of bright elements—anecdotes, facts, dramatic events—which are composed into a small story, which in turn is a segment of a larger story. It is important to realize that students' concepts of historical causality, and additional concepts of otherness, are still quite primitive. The history that engages them does so not because it is true and has determined our present forms of life and consciousness. Rather, it engages in so far as it entertains them and meets the requirements set out above. Students at the romantic stage have only the vaguest sense of history as a single and continuous process of which they and their world are a part.

An important principle, perhaps not ideally illustrated in the above examples, is that normally the further from the students' experience the element is with which the romantic association is formed, the more interest will be generated. To use a rather imprecise metaphor, it is a bit like a spark of electricity shooting across two terminals. The farther apart they are, the greater the energy generated to make the connection. Making a connection with something distant from students' experience creates a spark of intellectual energy that may by itself fuel interest for a considerable time. A great romantic writer like Mary Renault practices this constantly. She frequently begins with the unusual, the different, and connects us to it by means of transcendent human qualities—like courage and fortitude—with which we readily associate. In order to tell the exploits of Alexander in *The Persian Boy,* for example, she begins with the wholly alien world of a Persian eunuch, and, having connected us with this, she can provide a fresh perspective on what is to many a familiar story.

The obsessive fascination with detail once connection has been made with any topic must determine some of the learning activities that will form the middle of the story unit. The tendency to cover a body of material at a uniform level of detail must be resisted. At the romantic stage the student requires both a general context that generates a story form and that engages interest and an opportunity to fasten onto some area in minute detail. If one is teaching a unit on the Renaissance explorers, for example, it would be well not to be concerned solely with who went where when but to look in minute detail at how a ship was stocked, exactly how much and what kinds of food would be on board, what kind of people formed the crew, what were their backgrounds and expectations, what was the detailed structure of a typical ship, who slept where, what facilities and powers did each member of the crew have, and so on. One might want to compare in such exhaustive detail a ship and voyage of an English venturer, like Sir Francis Drake, with a Portugese or Spanish exploratory journey or with Christopher Columbus' voyage to America. This, of course, requires that the teacher make available the sources students can go to for this kind of information. Initially, the more attractive the source materials the better—Macaulay's books would provide ideal starting points—but once students become interested they will ransack the dullest sources with a sense of excitement that is fed rather than diminished by the dullness or relative inaccessibility of the source.

Frequently, when teaching about ancient Greece or Rome, teachers focus on those aspects of ancient life that have something in common with life today (for example, family life and homes) or with things that have left a direct and clear mark on the present (for example, words derived from Greek and Latin). Here again, a criterion for selecting what is to be studied in the past is what content students may be familiar with in the present. Some teachers who find these content associations trivial, argue that knowledge of ancient Greece and Rome is thus irrelevant to typical modern high-school students. Other teachers frequently defend the relevance of Greece and Rome on the grounds of these content associations with the modern world. My claim is that content has little to do with relevance, which may be achieved at this stage by romantic association with some transcendent human quality. And, to run the risk of overstating the point, the more alien the world with which students can be connected, the more relevant is knowledge about it to their educational development.

## CONCLUSION

We may characterize the romantic stage as that during which students explore the limits of the reality with which they have to deal. They do this primarily by focusing attention on extremes. They connect themselves with the extremes through the human qualities that most transcend the threats of everyday life—power, courage, nobility, beauty, genius, and all the old virtues.

The kind of curriculum this scheme leads to at this stage contrasts even more starkly than that at the mythic stage with typical expanding horizons curricula. The expanding horizons curricula are based on the assumption that students discover the world by progressively moving further outwards along lines of content associations, whereas the characteristics outlined here suggest that students explore reality by first making contact with its most extreme limits and then working inwards. I am claiming that all curricula that are composed on the assumption that students' knowledge of the world must be gradually extended on lines of content associations from the self and local experiences, perform an enormous disservice to students' educational development. They will also, incidently, bore most students out of their minds.

It is perhaps not surprising that this stage of intellectual wonder and excitement is also the stage of most acute boredom. If the mind is not caught up and flying in wonderful realms, it has to descend into the everyday world against which it has developed little conceptual defence. The mind at the romantic stage largely lacks the ability to derive much meaning from the everyday world. It does not yet know the context in which the everyday and commonplace are meaningful. For this reason alone, a curriculum that focuses on local matters ("How your city council works"; "Chemical reactions around the home"; "Local flora and fauna") is likely to drive most students to withdraw entirely. If they are literate, they will read westerns, love stories, or science fiction under the desk. If they are not, they will simply go catatonic or arrive in class stoned. My brutal claim is that those well-meaning teachers who try to engage students in what is relevant and assume that the relevant is to be found in their everyday environment are simply moving further in the direction of boring students and alienating them from their world.

Many scholars and teachers with a precise sense of how their discipline should be studied consider the kind of knowledge that engages students at the romantic stage in some way disreputable. Romantic-stage students seem like wide-eyed tourists interested only in the spectacular sights and bored by the background and detail that most interests scholars and teachers. Such teachers find their educational duty in ridiculing the romantic search for the extreme and the kind of knowledge that this entails, and they concentrate on trying to turn students into mini-researchers. It is hard to persuade some people that the immature require immature concepts and methods of inquiry and that this romantic engagement with the awesome, the wonderful, the different is not only acceptable but *necessary* for students' educational development.

I will discuss appropriate content for each stage in chapters 6 and 7, but want here to make one point about students' great ability to memorize and retain detail at this stage. Frequently in educational writing, memorization, or, pejoratively, rote learning, is depreciated, as though it is somehow necessarily incompatible with inquiry or exploration. Particularly, in recent decades, rote learning of poetry seems to have become educationally disreputable. Yet a mind stocked with fine poetry and prose enriches both the rhythms of one's language and the range of one's thought and sentiment and provides an infinitely rich treasure that can be drawn on at will through the rest of one's life. Similarly, a crude mass of factual knowledge about any discipline area (apart from being important for the best fulfillment of the next stage, as I shall show) has an important intellectual and aesthetic value. Only people without such treasures depreciate their value, and it is inappropriate to accept the advice and guidance of the ignorant in matters of education.

# 3

# THE PHILOSOPHIC STAGE

Approximate ages,
14/15 to 19/20 years

## CHARACTERISTICS
From romantic to philosophic

At the romantic stage, students' perception focuses on the extremes, on the most fascinating bits and pieces, on vivid true stories, on dramatic events and ideas, on bizarre facts, on heroes and heroines, and on some particular areas in great detail. There is of course the realization that all these are parts of the same world, but the connections between the parts are not a matter of much concern. Students connect themselves with these elements directly, by means of romantic associations. One aspect of the move from the romantic to the philosophic stage may be seen in the strengthening realization that all the bright bits and pieces are interconnected parts of some general *unit*. History, for example, is increasingly seen as less a set of stories, a set of styles of living, and more as a continuum of styles, a single complex story.

With students' perception of the world as a unit, in which everything is in some vague way related to everything else, comes the realization that they too are a part of the unit. Instead of retaining a romantic transcendence over the world, they come to realize that they are largely *determined* by their place in it. That is, students begin to sense that they are what they are, not as a matter of their romantic choices, but because the laws of nature, of human psychology, of social life, and of historical development apply to them as to everyone else. The direct romantic connections to the bright bits and pieces are dissolved in the growing realization that their proper connection to the world is by means of enormously complicated causal chains and networks. This shift involves the realization that they are not as free as they had thought; they are entrammeled in the world as in a spider's web.

As with the transition to the romantic stage, this is a period of critical educational importance. The relatively rapid decay of the romantic world view requires that students establish a new kind of intellectual security within this newly perceived world. To do this they have to establish their place and their roles in the natural, social, and historical *processes* of which they are becoming aware. From being transcendent players, they have to become *agents*.

The means whereby this new security is established follows from students' perception of themselves as parts of complex processes, that is, as parts of natural, social, and historical processes. If they are parts of complex processes then the way to understand their proper roles within the processes is to discover how these processes work. The major defining characteristic of the philosophic stage, then, is the search for *the* truth about human psychology, for *the* laws of historical development, for *the* truth about how societies function. That is, the philosophic focus is on the *general laws* whereby the world works. By having an understanding of how the world functions, the students will know their proper place and roles, and they will securely know themselves.

Whereas at the romantic stage students develop a sense of the limits of reality, a sense of its scope and scale, at the philosophic stage they turn inward, as it were, and conduct a general survey of the real world; they begin to chart a mental map of its general features. Again, this is not a process of expansion outwards along lines of content associations; rather, it is a closer charting of the context within which the student exists. It is not a further expansion *from* the self, but rather a closer approach *toward* the self.

### The craving for generality

In *Poetics,* Aristotle distinguishes between history on the one hand and poetry or fiction on the other, on the grounds that the former is concerned with establishing particular truths whereas the latter is concerned with more general or philosophic truths—the historian is concerned with whether this or that *happened* whereas the poet is concerned with what *happens* of necessity, with the general laws of things. It is on the basis of this distinction that I call this stage philosophic. Students' interest is little engaged by particular knowledge for its own sake; it is primarily engaged by the kinds of pursuits Aristotle thought proper to the poet, that is, finding very general truths about natural, social, psychological, or historical processes.

The endless particulars which students learn during the romantic stage and which are made meaningful by romantic association now threaten to be merely chaotic bits and pieces littering the mental landscape. To be made philosophically meaningful requires that they be organized within some general scheme. The first move of this mental map-making stage is to establish a sense of the main features of the world that is to be mapped.

To turn again to history for an example, at the philosophic stage, a student might be attracted by a fairly simple form of Marxism because it offers a means of readily organizing a vast range of particulars.[1] It provides an enormously general scheme by means of which *all* history, all the phenomena of the past (and present and future too) can be reduced from their unmanageable diversity to a

---

[1] I use this example, and will use it throughout this chapter, not to promote or denigrate Marxism, but because a typically unsophisticated Marxist perspective makes this point more dramatically than it might be made by taking the example of, say, a progressive liberal view of history, or a Toynbeean image of rising and falling organic civilizations.

relatively simple process. Once one understands the process, the laws of history, the details may be swept up, slotted into their places in the process, and be made meaningful. All that knowledge learned at the romantic stage about knights and peasants and the great artists of the Renaissance is suddenly endowed with a new meaning as part of the decay of feudalism and the rise of the bourgeoisie. That is, the *meaning* of the particulars is now derived *primarily* from their place within the general scheme.

Such a general scheme, which determines the meaning not only of the past but of the present and future as well, also provides students with a means of understanding their proper roles as agents within the historical process. If they accept the simple Marxist view, for example, they know that their proper role in Western societies should involve them in exacerbating the contradictions of capitalism, hindering the plans of reactionary bourgeois forces, and furthering the cause of the proletariat. If they accept a liberal progressive view, their roles as agents will involve them in defending and strengthening the liberal institutions of their society.

A further result of meaning being derived from the general view, is that the obsessive hobbies or collecting of the romantic stage tend to lose interest and be dropped.

## Ordering schemes

The philosophic craving for generality is the means whereby chaotic particular knowledge about the world is *reduced* to manageable proportions. This urge toward the general leads students to develop the abstract intellectual tools necessary for imposing order on the most complex processes.

Thus, quite suddenly, very general concepts—like society, culture, the mind, evolution, human nature—become prominent in students' language and thinking. The complex of social interactions, of institutions, of people and their jobs and families, of buildings and forms of transportation are reduced to concepts like society or culture, and may be juggled with a few equally general concepts to establish for the students enormously general principles about how the world works. From these concepts and principles, they form ideologies and metaphysical schemes; intellectual tools with which they can organize, simplify, and reduce even the greatest complexities with casual confidence. Ideologies and metaphysical schemes represent the boldest lines that give order to the students' mental map of the world. They become the fixed coordinates by means of which all particulars and details are located and given meaning.

Another reflection of this urge toward imposed order is the development of hierarchies. If one begins to appreciate music at this stage, the philosophic impulse is to ask who is *the best* composer, and who is the second best, the third best, and so on. The impulse at this stage is toward discovering the most powerful criterion that will allow one to organize all composers (or football players, or actors, or automobiles) by slotting them into place in a hierarchy. Frequently, this leads to the imposition of inappropriate single-criterion hierarchies where multiple-criteria should be applied.

For example, it does not make much sense to ask who is *the best* composer. Because of the nature of composers' activities, the different skills of two excellent composers cannot be compared on the grounds of any single criterion: $X$ may compose the best string quartets, but $Y$ may compose the best symphonies. $Z$, however, might compose the best string quartets in the sense that the best balance is achieved among the instruments; $P$ might be a better composer for the cello in string quartets, and so would be superior to $X$ in that respect. One can make increasingly sophisticated distinctions, until the notion of "best" on some single hierarchy becomes meaningless.[2]

The philosophic students' prime requirement, however, is to get some kind of control over the bewildering and threatening diversity of the subject under consideration. The philosophic impulse is to establish a first general ordering on *some* useful criterion. The refinements and sophistications can only follow an initial general ordering.

[2]It does, of course, make sense to ask who is one's favorite composer or football player. It is characteristic of this stage to confuse personal choice with an objective criterion of truth.

This search for the criteria by which things may be ranked in hierarchies is a development from, but also different from, the romantic collecting and organizing of something in great detail. The focus of interest at the philosophic stage moves from the particulars to the principles by which the particulars may be ordered. At the romantic stage, the particulars and their immediate relationships provide the focus of interest. The philosophic concern with recognizing the best composer is not a romantic search for extremes, rather it is a part of the philosophic search for a criterion whereby all composers can be ranked.[3]

Once one has identified *the right* criterion for evaluating and ranking composers—or comedians, or novels, or football players— once one has found the ideology that shows *the truth* about the historical process, one can feel confident in dealing with particular composers, or football players, or historical facts and events; it becomes a simple job of slotting them into place. A characteristic of students at the philosophic stage is to be confident, or over-confident, that they know the meaning of everything. Indeed, the abusive observation often made about students at this stage is that "they think they know everything." This is precisely so. They *do* think they know the true meaning of everything, even of things they have not yet learned. That is, they think they understand the general principles from which the meaning of particulars is derived; thus knowing *the truth* in general, learning and organizing the particulars is seen as essentially a trivial task.

Students at this stage often become impatient with learning further details and become contemptuous of those scholars who seem interested in particulars for their own sake. Such scholars are dismissed as "fact grubbing," as narrow-minded, and as blind to the greater scheme of things.

---

[3] This might seem a regression rather than a development. The philosophic generalizations might seem very crude and simpleminded compared with the complexity of the romantic organization of some subject. But it is the generation of very abstract philosophic ordering concepts that will eventually permit much more powerful and refined organization. Romantic stage organizing lacks the power of philosophic general schemes, and it lacks the potential for bringing diverse elements into complex processes.

Access to knowledge and
engagement of interest

At the romantic stage, students' prime means of access to knowledge
is by association with those things that help them feel transcendence
over the threatening complexity of the world. The prime means of
access to knowledge at the philosophic stage is a development from
this. Security now is sought not in transcending the world, but in
finding one's proper place within it, and this is discovered by
understanding *the truth* about the world. The primary association
at the philosophic stage, then, is *the Truth*.

Similarly, students' interest at the romantic stage is engaged by
those things that support a sense of transcendence. At the philosophic stage, students' interest is engaged primarily by the knowledge which helps "body forth"[4] the general schemes which they
identify as expressing the truth about historical, psychological,
social, or natural processes. For example, if one accepts the simple
Marxist ideology, then one's interest is focused by that onto the
particular knowledge that best clarifies and supports it.

The intellectual achievement that establishes the student in the
philosophic stage is the relatively rapid transition from romantic
interests to finding very general principles or laws. The success of
this transition turns on the power or sophistication of the general
principles or laws that the student generates.[5] The power or sophistication of the general principles turns largely on the amount
and variety of particular knowledge the student has which the
principles are generated to organize. This seems to lead to a most
unfashionable conclusion: to a significant degree, educational
development beyond the romantic stage depends on the student

---

[4] I use this term in the sense developed by F. M. Cornford in *Thucydides Mythistoricus*
(London: Edward Arnold, 1907).

[5] By *generates*, I don't mean that students formulate or originate such principles or
laws for themselves. There is, however, a sense in which students make the principles
their own by adopting them to the particular knowledge, values, attitudes and so on,
that individual students organize. *Generate* should be understood in this restricted
sense.

knowing a lot. That is, a sheer quantity of knowledge is educationally important.[6]

For example, if students know very little history, they may simply be unable to generate any principles or laws useful for imposing general order on the historical process. If they know equally little about other subjects and are able to generate only equally inadequate principles to organize them, they will lack the means to develop educationally beyond the romantic stage. That is to say, having enough knowledge to be able to generate from it some general vision of a complex process, some ideology, or metaphysical scheme, is a prerequisite for moving beyond the romantic stage and into the philosophic stage of educational development.

If students know some history—not a great deal, but have knowledge about a number of periods of history and of forms of life—then quite crude generalizations may be adequate to organize their knowledge. They may, for example, accept the truth of such general schemes as are expressed by: "the history of the world is the process that leads to more and more happiness for more and more people"; or "history is the process of destruction that follows from man getting out of harmony with nature." These are crude not because they are false or because they cannot organize a lot of knowledge, but because they can organize too much too easily.

If students have a great deal of knowledge, the generation of relatively sophisticated schemes will be demanded to coalesce the knowledge into some coherent process. It is not easy to express in few words examples of such schemes; however, one might cite the Marxist vision of dialectical development by means of class struggle, or the liberal focus on the gradual progress of those institutions that sustain bourgeois culture and bourgeois freedoms for increasing numbers of people.

Of course mere quantity of knowledge is insufficient to guar-

---

[6] A relatively large quantity of academic knowledge does not seem to play any equally significant role in the processes of moral, psychological, or social development, or even of that kind of development Piaget deals with. The fact that this principle is ignored in other developmental theories suggests, again, that their focus is not education.

antee a successful transition to the philosophic stage. The generation of sophisticated general schemes depends also on the *range* of knowledge that has to be coalesced. This suggests a further principle for teaching at the romantic stage. During the romantic stage, students tend to develop what might be called encyclopedic interests; they are drawn to quite widely divergent topics that have those characteristics described in the previous chapter. The unsympathetic description of students at this stage is that they are scatterbrained; they seem to lack any sustained ability for study of particular topics, except with regard to their obsessions in which their engagement seems disproportionate. They also lack any strong need to establish connections between the diverse bodies of romantic knowledge that they gather. That is, like an encyclopedia, they can maintain separate bodies of knowledge without attempting to establish logical relationships among them. Given the above observation about the requirements for successful transition to the philosophic stage, this scatterbrained gathering of divergent knowledge should be encouraged during the romantic stage. The more varied the knowledge students gather, the more complex and sophisticated will have to be the philosophic scheme they generate to weave all the diverse pieces into a single, or a few, processes.

Educational development *through* the philosophic stage may be characterized in terms of the increasing sophistication of the students' general schemes. What causes the schemes to become increasingly sophisticated? Primarily, *more* knowledge, because the *lack* of a considerable body of knowledge *is* sufficient to guarantee an inability to develop educationally beyond the romantic stage.

It is the constant interaction between general scheme and particular knowledge that fuels, as it were, the student's development through this stage. The general scheme demands further knowledge to clarify it, the further knowledge demands refinements and revisions in the general scheme, which in turn requires further knowledge to more fully body forth the newly refined or revised vision. The fuel of this process is nothing less than the difference between reality and the general scheme which seeks to mirror it. Between reality and the idea lies the fuel of philosophic inquiry.

Why does not the particular knowledge simply body forth the

general scheme satisfactorily, and so not fuel constant further inquiry? Because additional particular knowledge will usually contain what I will call *anomalies* for the general scheme. The more knowledge the student acquires, the more likely it is to generate anomalies, and so require revisions in the general scheme, which in turn will require further inquiry, the accumulation of yet more knowledge, which in turn will contain further anomalies, which will lead to increasingly sophisticated general schemes.

What is an anomaly in this context? If, for example, a student developed a fairly simple Marxist view of the historical process and looked for particular knowledge to support it, things like the modern persistence and growth of western bourgeois societies or the apparent survival and enrichment of some of the English landed aristocracy during the seventeenth century present anomalies. To account for the knowledge the student acquires about these seeming exceptions need not destroy the general scheme; such knowledge will normally lead to a more sophisticated Marxist vision. To use different language, one might say that the growth of particular knowledge sets up a dissonance that can only be corrected by altering the general scheme.

Again, I need to qualify somewhat my claim about a simple quantity of knowledge being needed for development through this stage. In addition, knowledge that is anomalous, or creates dissonance, to the student's general schemes is most valuable. I want to defend my insistence on the need for a large quantity of knowledge because a critical mass of knowledge is required to get the dialectical process between general scheme and particular knowledge moving, and a good deal of further knowledge is required to keep it going.

Above, I have described the process in very general and ideal terms. Normally, of course, students at the philosophic stage have a considerable stake in their general scheme—the stake being their intellectual security—and they resist changing it. Indeed, it takes some confidence and security to be willing to even refine, let alone revise, a general scheme. This observation suggests a principle for teaching: that one should first encourage a student to securely develop a general scheme before introducing anomalies that will challenge its adequacy as a *true* account of the process. (I will consider this, and other implications for teaching and learning, in the examples at the end of this chapter.)

One of the problems that follows from accumulating only a relatively small amount, and range, of knowledge at the romantic stage (consequently generating only very crude general schemes at the transition to the philosophic stage) is that very crude general schemes hinder the process whereby anomalies lead to increasing sophistication. The problem with a crude general scheme is not that it does not organize enough knowledge, but rather that it can organize anything. If it is crude enough, everything becomes evidence to support it and nothing challenges it. With such crude general schemes formed at the critical transition stage, students may thereafter increase their knowledge, but that knowledge will not force revision and sophistication of their general scheme and so will contribute nothing to increased understanding. Such knowledge will tend to remain, to use Whitehead's term, "inert." In cases like this, students will establish only a toehold, as it were, in the philosophic stage. Their primary interest in knowledge will remain romantic.

The ideal teachers of students entering the philosophic stage must be sensitive to the beginning signs of generalizing; they must then encourage students to develop general ideologies and metaphysical schemes that will seem simplistic and perhaps even obnoxious; they must sympathetically deal with students' overconfidence and perhaps even their intellectual contempt; they must be ready to support them at those moments of fearful insecurity when their ideologies or metaphysical schemes threaten to be inadequate; and they must gradually introduce anomalies and dissonance at appropriate times, encouraging greater sophistication in the students' general schemes. So easily written.

## Philosophic stories

From the above description of the characteristics of students' thinking at this stage, it may seem that the story form plays no significant role in their organizing of knowledge. But there does remain, I think, a significant feature of the story form. What we see in moving from the mythic to the romantic to the philosophic stage is a reduction in the simplicity and determining force of the story form. Although the form is so weakened by the philosophic stage that we do not normally recognize it, exposing its persisting force seems important because of the implications for organizing material so that it is best understood and used by students.

As shown above, the story form is different from reality in that it *ends*; reality goes on, and we are in "the middest." An important feature of typical philosophic generalized schemes is that they create a unit out of disparate pieces; conceptualizing a process requires the imposition of some beginning and end. This may be seen most clearly with regard to history. In order to conceive of history as a single process, the student has to apply a kind of plot to it. Marxism, for example, sees history as a dialectical struggle of classes with conflicting interests that will finally be resolved in a classless society. That "finally" is important. Inherent in the description of the process is the assertion of how it will end. Similarly, other philosophic ideologies imply how the process will eventually unfold.

The function of imposing an end, as discussed earlier, is to be able to impose determinate meaning on the elements that make up the process. By knowing that there *will* be a dictatorship by the proletariat, the Marxist knows the *true* meaning of class conflict in the past and present. The confidence (overconfidence) about knowing the true meaning of things is achieved by use of the central feature of the story.[7]

One may get a clearer notion of some of the characteristics of this stage by examining the kinds of stories or literature that most appeal to philosophic students. In general, one might describe it as primarily a literature of ideas. In the previous chapter, I mentioned that most science fiction has a romantic appeal, but there is also a body of science fiction that has in addition a philosophic appeal. Typically, it does not simply tell stories made strange by projection

[7] Again, while this characteristic of philosophic thinking may seem more relevant to the study of history than to physics, in chapter 7, I will show how it is no less relevant to the sciences and other curriculum areas.

into the future, but implicitly examines some aspect of society by extrapolation—by relating it to the present by some causal mechanism. That is, such philosophic science fiction does not create different worlds, but examines ideas about this world by extending them into a possible future, or an alternative present, or even an altered past. A writer like Jorge Luis Borges exemplifies this stage quite precisely. His brief "Inquisitions" involve primarily a play with ideas; there is a relative absence of exploring human motivations and character. Typically, philosophic literature is poor in its representation of individual human variety. People tend to be types and their role is to give movement to, or embody, the ideas.

Philosophic games and stories tend to become fused. As students become agents in the stories or the causal processes they perceive in the world, they convert the stories into games in which they play a role. These more grown up stories/games tend to be taken very seriously and, as St. Augustine noted, are often called "business." In his *Confessions* (Book 1:10), he concludes, "I cannot believe that a good judge would approve of the beatings I received as a boy on the ground that my games delayed my progress in studying subjects which would enable me to play a less creditable game later in life." It is the imposition of general schemes that reduce reality and assert clear rules and roles which gives life at the philosophic stage the quality of a game. We see these serious games players all around us, immature adults acting out roles in their self-limited reality. They tend to make an absolute separation between their serious roles—as businessperson, revolutionary, or whatever—and their recreational activities.

## Narcissism

I mentioned above that this stage does not so much represent a further expansion of horizons distant from the self, but rather a closer approach toward the self. A person's educational development, I have suggested, is a process whose focus of interest and intellectual engagement begins with little concern for reality, with a mythlike construction of the world; then romantically establishes the boundaries and extent of reality; and then, at the philosophic stage, maps the general features of the real world in terms of very general organizing grids. At the philosophic stage, students recognize themselves as parts of complex processes, and they set about establishing the truth about these processes with some psychological urgency, because in establishing the truth about the processes, they discover the truth about themselves.

In the sense that students' interest in the world is primarily directed not toward finding out about the world for its own sake, but rather for their sakes—to establish a sense of their own identity—I call this stage *narcissistic*. Indeed, in this sense, the two previous stages are also narcissistic, but it is at the philosophic stage that this narcissism, this concern for knowledge because of what it tells about oneself, becomes most acute and evident.

The prime function of the craving for generality, then, is not simply to organize knowledge about the world; this powerful impulse derives primarily from students' needs to define and know themselves. They look at the world as they would a mirror, to see themselves. It is a period during which those academic subjects which seem to promise most direct knowledge about the self become attractive, for example, psychology, sociology, anthropology, and today for women, women's studies, and for blacks, black studies. Students' interest in "primitive" people, for example—to the despair of many anthropology teachers—is directed by their desire to know what about *themselves* is determined by culture and what is their basic human genetic endowment, there is little concern left over for the uniqueness of the people being studied. If the teaching of these subjects, and of history too, treats the search for general laws and huge explanatory schemes as misguided, philosophic students quickly become disenchanted and lose interest.

We may see this philosophic desire to simplify and reduce the complexity of the world into general processes that locate the self as an immature and unfruitful method of inquiry. It is difficult to persuade the mature teacher that this philosophic stage is not simply a fault to be corrected as quickly as possible. Again, immaturity is not a fault in the immature. This kind of law seeking, this philosophic focus on the very general and contempt for the mere particular and the "fact grubber", is a *necessary* stage in a person's educational development. One does not develop by avoiding it or suppressing it; it contributes something of importance to the mature educated person, i.e., the search for the recurrent, for regularities, for essences, for general order. One does not dispense with this, one learns gradually to control it. During the philosophic stage students are more controlled by general ideas than they are in control of them. One develops by going *through* this stage; the general schemes becoming increasingly sophisticated until, as I shall describe at the beginning of the next chapter, they break down as inadequate in the face of the infinite richness and uniqueness of the particulars of the world. One can, however, achieve an ordered sense of the world's rich particularity, only *after* first imposing some general initial ordering scheme on it. This is what is achieved during the philosophic stage of educational development.


## TEACHING AND LEARNING AT THE
## PHILOSOPHIC STAGE


I have suggested that students at this stage have little interest in particular knowledge for its own sake, and yet I have argued that the accumulation of large amounts of particular knowledge is necessary to work through this stage. There may seem to be a problem here: how are students to be engaged in learning a lot of particular knowledge if it has no intrinsic interest for them?

The resolution of this problem at the philosophic stage follows from the nature of the dialectical process of interaction between general scheme and particular knowledge that I have outlined above. Though particular knowledge has no *intrinsic* interest for students, the psychologically vital need to develop general schemes requires the accumulation of particular knowledge to give them substance. That is, accumulating particular knowledge will become vitally important to students if it can be seen as useful in building and elaborating their general schemes.

We talk about children's and students' natural desire to know about the world. But the focus of their desire for knowledge changes through the process of their development. The interests of the six-year-old child are different from those of the sixteen-year-old student, and each age group makes sense of the world and their experiences differently. Teaching requires sensitivity to these differences. Each stage of their educational development represents a different expression of their natural desire to know about the world, and satisfying that desire requires a clear sense of *how* knowledge needs to be organized and made accessible so that students at the different stages can best be engaged by knowledge and *use* it for their further development.

Teaching at the philosophic stage requires a clear sense of how the dialectical process of interaction between general scheme and particular knowledge begins and keeps going. Ideally, the process is a natural one, given exposure to the proper environment. But ideal circumstances are rarely available. The teacher's job is to intervene where necessary to assist the process toward the ideal: to direct students toward the kind of knowledge that will best feed the development of their general scheme, or to help elaborate their general scheme so that it will best organize their particular knowledge.

At the risk of oversimplifying, I have characterized educational development through this stage as a kind of engine whose motive force is provided by the constant interaction between general and particular. The teacher's function—to continue this rather imprecise metaphor—is that of a regulator, ensuring that the proper balance between general and particular in the fuel keeps the engine chugging forward. Being able to perform this function properly presupposes that the teacher will have passed through this stage.

Acting as a regulator of the process of philosophic development is the most general principle for teaching that follows from the characterization of the stage. In addition, a few subsidiary principles may be derived from other characteristics touched on above. It was noted that students still require a loose kind of story form—a teleological implication— to provide a general context that allows them to ascribe clear philosophic meaning to whatever is being learned.

In teaching history, one way of providing this is by projecting the general scheme used to organize the particulars into the future to some end. If it is a scheme of liberal progress, for example, the student may be asked to speculate on what the historical process is progressing toward. This also allows the present to be located in the process, which gives students a means of deciding their proper roles as social agents. This present-oriented concern serves also to assist philosophic students' educational narcissism. History is perceived as a causal network, of which they form a part; their primary interest is in clarifying that part.[8]

The requirement that anomalies be generated to force revision and complication of the general scheme, leads to the principle of specialization. This returns us to the apparent paradox of this stage: despite the fact that students' primary focus of interest is on general schemes, it is the most specialized and particularistic inquiries that both feed the general scheme and fuel the process that will, eventually, lead the student beyond the belief in such schemes. Sensitivity and knowledge are required for the teacher to be able to guide students to specialize in a topic that, first, attracts students because it will help "body forth" their general scheme and, second, will produce the kinds of anomalies that will best ensure revision and elaboration of their general scheme.

The first question to ask when designing a unit for students at this stage, then, is "What is philosophic about the subject matter?" or "How is it organized when we look at it from a philosophic perspective?" That is, we will seek to organize the knowledge in a manner that will permit students at the philosophic stage to best use it for their further educational development.

Let us consider how the principles outlined above might affect the organization of knowledge about the Industrial Revolution. Following this, the kind of unit that best contributes to educational

---

[8] I know that I am here advocating what many history teachers at colleges and universities most dislike. This narcissistic present- or future-oriented concern seems to them one of the most nefarious characteristics of students, one to which they bend all their efforts to eradicate. I agree that, in a mature scholar, such an attitude would be nefarious. My claim, however, is that it is a stage through which students have to pass. In the next chapter, I will discuss how to get them beyond this stage.

development at this stage will be sketched, and a few more principles for teaching will be considered after the examples. Again, I do not intend to draw up detailed units or lesson plans here, but rather to indicate how the above principles affect the general organization of and access to knowledge.

*Example 3.1  The Industrial Revolution*   What patterns emerge when we look at the Industrial Revolution from a philosophic perspective? The Marxist perspective which I have used as an example throughout this chapter may again be considered briefly to clarify the general form beginning such a unit. To the Marxist, the important focus on—and the *meaning* of—the Industrial Revolution derives from its place within the yet wider context of the dialectical process of history which is seen in the thesis, antithesis, and synthesis of class struggles. In very general terms, the Industrial Revolution is the rise to dominance of the bourgeois class whose creation of wealth stimulated the formation and growth to consciousness of the proletarian class, whose interests were antithetical to those of the bourgeoisie.

If this is the most general meaning of the Industrial Revolution from the Marxist point of view, attention is focused by this general scheme on those details that will best body it forth and show it to be the truth. That is, the general scheme determines what kinds of details are relevant and interesting. The Marxist is focused toward knowledge about: the mechanisms whereby bourgeois entrepreneurs created their wealth and developed the factory system; the rise of labour unions and the growth of proletarian self-consciousness; the conflicts between workers and managers; the alienation of workers from the products of their labors; the alienation that resulted from workers being considered less as people than as cogs of a machine for creating wealth; the colonization and exploitation of the non-industrialized world in the search for raw materials and markets. Detailed knowledge about these things is sought, primarily, because it will give body to the general scheme and will help Marxist students understand more securely their role in the historical process and modern society.

Let us look in a little more detail at another example. The two most general schemes used in organizing the historical process into some kind of unit are the *comic* and the *tragic*. The comic asserts that history is a process of improvement, of progress; the tragic declares that it is a process of decline, leading to destruction. Let us arbitrarily take the comic scheme that underlies a typical liberal humanitarian progressive view. (Marxism, of course, is also a comic scheme.)

It is important that the general scheme be made explicit and be developed adequately to provide a clear understanding of a general context for the Industrial Revolution. It is important to remember that at the philosophic stage meaning always derives from the more general, filtering down level by level, as it were, to the most particular. If the particulars are not connected to the general, they will be largely meaningless to the student, because the student is connected to the general; that is, the students' access to the particular is through the general.

We will begin our unit on the Industrial Revolution with a sketch of the general scheme. This may be done by any means or media the teacher may wish to use; it may be introduced as simply a speculation: "Some people see history as a process in which knowledge and reason have been gradually, but increasingly, applied to the regulation of political and social life for the greatest good of the greatest number. . . . " Such a general scheme is one we are quite familiar with in the western democracies. It focuses attention on the story of "the advance of civilization" that we often accept without thinking. Sketching this for students would be easy for most of us, making it dramatic and fresh might require the use of media or narrative talents. It is a story that imposes its own beginning—in the middle east; gets going with ancient Greece and Rome; stutters into the Dark Ages when nothing much of any significance happened (except perhaps Irish monks and Alcuin at Charlemagne's court); Peter Abelard leads us into the cathedrals, universities, and the High Middle Ages; and then we are back onto the main track with the Renaissance, the Enlightenment, and that nineteenth-century explosion of creative energy, of which the Industrial Revolution is a part. Our focus will be directed on political organizations that allowed the products of cultural life to survive and to feed following generations; on the origins and growth of liberal institutions; on the rule of law and the means of enforcing law to provide security of life and property to the citizenry and to expand their freedoms.

Thus, when we come to the Industrial Revolution, we have created a context which determines where its meaning is to be found; we are focused toward those aspects of the Industrial Revolution that show the further advance of this liberal progressive process. Typically, this leads to a concern with the abuses against what we have come to consider as individuals' rights and with the legal and other machinery developed to eliminate those abuses. Consequently, the following concerns become central: child labor, the hours put in by factory workers, threats against the social order brought on by abuses of rights, and the legislation enacted to ease or eradicate the abuses. In addition, factories, inventions, and processes of production become important as the creators of the wealth that sustains and aids the development of cultural activities, the discovery and propagation of knowledge, and other uses of reason and humane intelligence.

These concerns, then, will provide the content for our initial view of the Industrial Revolution. This initial rundown should not try to engage students in learning details. Rather it should serve primarily as a reiteration of the general liberal progressive scheme at a somewhat low level of generality. Learning details of particular British Acts of Parliament or of production statistics of American farms and factories too soon will simply disconnect those details from the general scheme—which is the only meaningful access students have to them at this stage. The initial rundown is not to challenge but to reinforce the general scheme.

Once the students have developed a general overview of the Industrial Revolution within the context of the progressive liberal scheme—a sense of the pattern of labor abuses and corrective legislation, the role of the abolition of slavery, the nature of the reactionary opposition, the main characters, movements, and organizations, all embellished with occasional romantic facts and details[9]—the next step is to develop some flexibility in the students' understanding of the general scheme.

One might have the students consider questions like the following: Is industrialization fundamentally at odds with natural human behavior, or human nature? Has industrialization taken on a life of its own, Frankenstein-like, which now threatens its creators? Is industrialization doing more good then harm? Is it out of control? Why should this contribution to reasoned progress lead, in civilized countries, to Hitler, Moussolini, and Stalin, with enormous and enthusiastic popular support? Do we face such dangers in our country?

What do such questions achieve? First, it does not much matter that students do not have enough data to be able to formulate adequate answers. No one has. The purpose is to stimulate some *movement* in the general scheme; students must apply the scheme to new (very general) data, trying to impose shape and pattern on complex historical phenomena. Teachers should encourage argument and discussion at this point, to help students clarify their scheme, to help clarify how and where students disagree in applying their schemes, to help clarify for students what they believe. Once the students show some flexibility and control over the general scheme and some kind of commitment to their *own* perspectives, then the teacher may begin the further descent toward the particular, to kick into self-sustaining life, so to speak, the engine of philosophic inquiry.

Deciding how this is to be done is the point at which the teacher's sensitivity and knowledge are at a premium. A means of engaging students in some detailed area of inquiry about the Industrial Revolution that will first elaborate their individual general scheme and then will raise anomalies in the scheme is required. For example, if a student has adopted a simple Marxist general scheme, she may be asked to examine in detail the movement to abolish

[9]I will consider the persistence of romantic elements in the philosophic stage and its implications for teaching in chapter 5.

slavery and to see how it can be made to support her scheme; she might be asked to focus on the connections and conflicts between the interests of those who supported and profited from industrialization and of those who supported the abolition of slavery. If a student has adopted a simple liberal progressive general scheme, he may be asked to consider what was the main motive, or dynamic, that produced legislation to improve working conditions; he might be asked to focus on whether such legislation was enacted *only* when it was seen as supporting rather than threatening increased production.

Such assignments encourage students to gather knowledge that may be used to support their general schemes, but which will also generate knowledge that is anomalous. If the teacher is successful in finding the question and topic that engages the individual student's interest, then the dialectical process of anomalies causing revision of the general scheme which then demands further knowledge to better body it forth gets underway. Ideally, the teacher may more or less withdraw at this point and let the student get on with it. The teacher's role then will be just to regulate the balanced growth between sophistication of the general scheme and accumulating knowledge.

If the dialectical movement appears to splutter and break down, the teacher needs to intervene, either to ask further probing philosophic questions[10] which better help to body forth the general scheme or which better raise more pointed anomalies, or to introduce a more sophisticated general scheme that can better organize the particular knowledge whose anomalies may have undermined a previous general scheme.

As the student develops through the philosophic stage, the teacher's role increasingly becomes one of raising anomalies to the general scheme. This is a better procedure than challenging the student's general scheme head to head with another scheme. If

---

[10] A phrase like "asking questions" is not to be taken as a literal description of method. For economy's sake, I am not discussing here the variety of methods and techniques available to teachers. For "asking questions," the reader should imagine any kind of assignment or interaction with students that best achieves this end.

the teacher is a powerful advocate for the alternative, it might have either of the equally bad effects of persuading the student to accept it as true—undergoing a conversion experience—or driving the student to an excessive commitment in defence of his or her own general scheme. The prime aim of teaching at this stage is to assist each student to develop an increasingly sophisticated general scheme. In their increasing sophistication, as I will discuss in the following chapter, lies the seeds of their own destruction.

One must remember that students are less interested in the Industrial Revolution than in themselves. Of particular interest to students as they inquire into the Industrial Revolution are those general historical processes that seem to be caused by, or follow from, personal motives. The historical role of individuals is interesting and important to students at this stage, not in the sense of romantic heroes and heroines causing events, but in the way people interact with the process. The above question about whether or not the humanitarian legislation can be accounted for by industrialists' self-interest rather than as resulting from humanitarian impulses raises this issue. Students who inquire into this question use history to enlighten something about themselves. At the romantic stage, students presuppose that they would do the noble thing and associate with those they take as heroes and heroines. At the philosophic stage, this presupposition is being undermined; students are motivated to discover just what is the truth about human behavior in general. For example, is self-interest the dynamic of liberal progress, rather than selflessness?

Having achieved a successful dialectical movement in this stage, the teacher may concentrate on widening as well as deepening students' knowledge of the Industrial Revolution. If the question about the dynamic of social change has proved a useful means of getting the process moving for a particular student, the same question may be applied to different phenomena. If a student's general scheme resists accommodating the conclusion that self-interest is the main dynamic of historical change, that student may be asked to study in detail various inventions, their adoption, and their proliferation to discover if any other dynamic but self-interest is able to explain the findings of the student's inquiry. Or, if the student has accepted that people's self-interest is the only motivator of historical events, that student may be asked to study in detail the activities of Robert Owen, Elizabeth Frye, and some of the middle-class supporters of the Chartists to discover if there is no distinction in terms of self-interest to be made between their behavior and that of the most ruthless mill-owners.

Let us turn briefly to the kind of unit that would be very useful in encouraging development through this stage.

*Example 3.2 Metahistories*  Rather than impose a particular general scheme on students, as the above example suggests, it would be better to provide them with exposure to a variety of schemes from which they might choose one, or combine features of a number of schemes that seem most suitable to best organizing their romantic knowledge.

An important principle for such a unit is that the various schemes should not be simply laid out dispassionately as a kind of smorgasbord, as all equivalent and equivalently false, the way an athiest might study comparative religions. The students may be expected to make a commitment to the truth of one, or a composite of their own making, so they must be presented as important and conflicting theories about the historical process—which is, after all, what they are.

The unit could be divided into sections, each one of which outlines, elaborates, and then applies a general scheme. One might begin with a Thucydidean notion of history as a tragic process, in which, human nature being what it is, political harmony will always be undermined by greed, self-deception, and folly, and destruction will result. An outline of Thucydides' account of the fall of Athens could introduce the section. With selected readings from his *History* one could present his image of the Periclean farsighted moderation that led to Athens' glory; then the crazy ambitions of Cleon and Alcibiades which led to its destruction in the campaign that finished so unbearably in the harbour at Syracuse. With the use of media, one could vivify the movement of armies and shifts of alliances and power. Role playing of crucial speeches to the Athenian *Agora* and the terrible Melian dialogue can bring life and drama to the ancient conflict between Athens and Sparta. This needs to be organized to emphasize Thucydides' philosophic message about the historical process.

Having developed a clear sense of the tragic general scheme, students may be asked to consider whether it is true of some other complex historical event, like the fall of the Roman Empire. That is, one must first choose to elaborate students' sense of the general scheme by using it to organize a phenomenon that may be fairly easily fitted to it. Thereafter, students may be asked to consider how far it is true of any other civilization they may wish to examine.

In similar fashion, other sections of the unit might consider a Rankean notion of a God-guaranteed progress of nation-states toward greater power and harmony; a Toynbeean image of rising and falling organic civilizations; an Hegelian/Marxist image of dialectical progress through class struggle; a Spencerian evolution; a Spenglerian vision of the declining west. A teacher could choose among these or other general schemes.

In addition, the teacher might throw in the occasional enormously general philosophic idea. For example, civilization may be seen as the product of some kind of energy whose center has been traveling westward around the world at increasing speed. It began slowly, moving from China, through India to the ancient middle eastern empires, then passed on to Egypt, then to Greece, and the Roman empire. After the fall of Rome, it passed to the Frankish Empire, and then to the most westerly European empires of Spain and England. They drove westward to the Americas, and their decline saw the rise in power of the eastern part of North America. More quickly than it moved through Europe, it passed across the continent to the west coast. The teacher may ask students how well such an idea fits history, what it means, what kind of energy it is, and whether the focus of energy seems due to reach China again in the near future. Similar ideas might involve seeing the development of civilization from the perspective of weather cycles, food production, and epidemics and control of diseases. A focus on the dynamic of historical change will always stimulate philosophic interest.

Such metahistories should always focus on the nature of man as a historical animal, his role in the causal network of events; they should also allow speculation and projection into the future, and concentration on the *meaning* of the present in each scheme. After each presentation of a scheme, students should be assigned to apply it to some other area of history. Debate, argument, discussion among students should be encouraged. Once students develop a commitment to some general scheme, they should be asked the kind of probing question about some particular historical event or period that will stimulate the dialectical interaction that will carry them through this stage.

Teaching at the philosophic stage has four critical points. The first comes with the transition to the stage, at which point students begin to formulate from their romantic knowledge some very general scheme or schemes. The teacher can best help this process with a unit like the one outlined in example 3.2.

The second critical step is to encourage the development of flexibility and commitment to the general scheme. Perceiving that the general scheme can be applied to, or imposed on, a variety of phenomena provides the student with greater security and encourages a greater commitment to it as a means of organizing and making philosophic sense of the world.

Third, the teacher needs to be sensitive to just what kind of question, assignment, or stimulus to inquiry will engage students in acquiring that knowledge which will best support their general scheme and also generate anomalies which will require some revision of the general scheme. (Piaget's notions of schemata assimilating and accommodating to new experiences or knowledge seems to be the most sophisticated and clear expression of the *process* I am referring to.) The teacher's task is to persist in stimulating inquiry in particular topics until the dialectical interaction gets properly underway.

Fourth, when the dialectical interaction is underway, the teacher's task is that of a regulator of the process, remaining sensitive to the developing sophistication of general schemes and the kind of knowledge students are seeking, to body them forth more fully. The teacher should be ready to intervene to support the developmental process whenever it seems in danger of running down. By this stage—which seems not to be reached by most students these days until their university careers have begun—students can be much more self-directed in their learning of particulars.

## CONCLUSION

The distinction between the romantic and philosophic stages of educational development finds no analogue in Piaget's or Erikson's developmental theories. It does, however, reflect a distinction recognized by Plato in his scheme of educational development. He distinguishes between a stage where the child has access to *dianoia*, a level of abstract thinking which, nevertheless, lacks the systematic generalizing characteristic of his next stage, *noesis*. Indeed, Plato's developmental stages—*eikasia, pistis, dianoia, noesis*[11]—seem to me quite analogous to my *mythic, romantic, philosophic,* and *ironic* stages. (This is a topic I deal with elsewhere.)

Erikson discusses the development of ideological schemes as a part of his "identity versus role confusion" stage.[12] I have already associated some aspects of this developmental task with my romantic stage. I am suggesting that an educational perspective on development will perceive an important distinction where a psychological or psycho-social perspective may make none. (Piaget, too, makes no such distinction within his stage of formal operations.)[13] For example, Erikson does not distinguish any sequence within his

[11] Plato *Republic* 6. 509–11 (trans. Francis MacDonald Cornford, New York: Oxford University Press, 1945), pp. 221–26.

[12] See Erik H. Erikson, *Childhood and Society*, 2d ed. (New York: W. W. Norton, 1963), ch. 8.

[13] See, for example, the final chapter of Bärbel Inhelder and Jean Piaget, *The Growth of Logical Thinking*, trans. Anne Parsons and Stanley Milgram (London: Routledge and Kegan Paul, 1958).

fifth stage for the acquisition of time perspective, role-experimentation, and the formation of ideologies. Observation of educational development, however, suggests that it is not until later in adolescence that growing mastery of abstract concepts coalesces into full ideological and metaphysical schemes.

In stressing the educational importance of students developing general schemes, I may have given the impression that any scheme, ideology, or metaphysical belief is equally good. My first four chapters, however, describe an ideal development through the stages, and so *presuppose* that students will go on to the next stage, in which they will outgrow their philosophic dependence on and belief in general schemes. That is, as long as the general schemes are crutches that will be discarded, if they adequately perform their philosophic function, then their particular characteristics are not *very* important, and it does not greatly matter what schemes students form commitments to. But if students do not develop beyond this stage, this casual unconcern is inappropriate. If they remain in the philosophic stage, and continue to believe in *the truth* of their ideology, for example, and use it to guide their social and political behavior, then in practice it matters critically what that ideology is.

I have mentioned Marxism frequently in this chapter, perhaps almost seeming to recommend it as a valuable tool for teaching history. But if one can be sure students will develop beyond the philosophic stage, then indeed Marxism can be a powerful general scheme that will contribute toward their educational development. If one cannot be sure that students will develop beyond this stage, then, to put it as unevaluatively as possible, such an ideology is inappropriate for best functioning within, and supporting the harmonious development of, western democratic societies. In as far as teachers have a choice in the general schemes their students adopt—and they can have to a considerable extent—an evolutionary liberal humanitarian ideology would probably be as useful as any to encourage.

This may seem a cynical, or authoritarian, or even immoral attitude—suggesting that we impose ideologies on students in the name of education. And to make matters worse, I have earlier recommended that we encourage students to become narcissistic, censorious, bullheaded, know-it-alls. I am clearly on dangerous ground. But education is a dangerous business. Only the simple-minded consider it simple. It is never a non-committal, uncommitted, value-free, flaccid, or bloodless enterprize. Activities in some of our "educational" institutions may be all these—but, if so, such activities are not educational. Being on dangerous ground, then, is a necessary condition for dealing with important educational issues.

The recommendations I am making about the issues raised in this chapter are doubly dangerous, because they conflict with some of the dominant attitudes found among educators today. We tend to resist anything that seems to impose values on students and try to avoid ideology and metaphysical beliefs wherever possible. It is no coincidence that the most popular innovations in curriculum are those which seem to offer teachers ways of approaching the directing of students' learning without having to accept responsibility for the particular direction it goes in. Many people are propagating techniques of value clarification, for example, which are based on what is to me a transparently absurd—though rarely explicit—notion of children and students having somehow within them autonomously held values which are elicited or clarified by the teacher's value-free questioning and encouragement.

Why such movements are so popular at present is not my concern here, but it is appropriate to note that they have in common the removal from the educator of the responsibility for making what should be educational, i.e., necessarily value-laden decisions. To believe that it is possible to educate in a value-free way is like believing it is possible to be in love unemotionally. I raise all this here because at the philosophic stage, contentious value issues, ideologies, metaphysical beliefs are properly not just inconvenient incidentals, but rather the central focus of education.

I am reacting here against what I see as a foolish excess of humanistic ideology, which leads to such diffidence about a teacher's right to interfere in children's and students' education that necessary guidance is not given. The danger of any reaction, of course, is that it will be read as promoting the opposite—in this case, a call for ruthlessly imposing values, ideologies, and metaphysical beliefs on children. I am not advocating this.

My claim is that forming an ideology, for example, represents entry to a necessary stage in a person's educational development. Educating students thus entails helping them enter and work through this stage; teachers have to help students make strong commitments to ideas that will seem simplistic, but which the teachers must take seriously. The immature will of necessity make immature commitments. One cannot educate students at this stage if one avoids the dangerous level of abstract general schemes where philosophic students locate truth.

In order to educate students at this stage, teachers must be at a more advanced stage of educational development. If teachers or professors have not developed beyond the philosophic stage and if they promote their general schemes as the truth, then they are ideologizing students not educating them. Even if they are diffident about propagating their own general schemes, they will be unable to direct students properly to attend to anomalous particulars, because they themselves locate truth, immaturely, in very general abstract schemes. Only if teachers and professors introduce students to general schemes knowing how to help them get beyond reliance on such schemes can they claim to be educating. It may, of course, happen that students will independently get beyond belief in an ideology to which a philosophic teacher has introduced them, but this is largely a matter of chance.

Yet again, this is a dangerous business. There is never a guarantee that a student will not for one reason or another get stuck at this philosophic stage; that the interaction between particular reality and abstract general scheme will not break down. One may generally characterize the two most common results of such a failure. If the general scheme fades and fails to direct inquiry into and the organization of particulars, one often gets a kind of mindless pedantry, which cannot distinguish the important from the trivial. If the general scheme becomes too powerful and is not affected by particulars, one has the often more dangerous situation in which ideas are more real than reality. This breeds ideologues, to whom human suffering is irrelevant, and all that matters is the cause, or to metaphysical beliefs that propose, for example, an afterlife or a deeper reality than the everyday, in comparison to which, again, everyday human suffering is discounted as meaningless. These extremes may be summed up in the words of W. H. Auden in his poem "Numbers and Faces": the person whose general scheme fails, tends to go "benignly potty" among particulars from which nothing is built; the person whose general scheme overshadows reality tends to go "horribly mad", imposing a crude single criterion of truth and value on the multifarious world.

A common fault of teaching at this stage is to attempt to persuade students, either aggressively or sympathetically, that their general schemes are false. To ask, for example, whether the Marxist scheme is true or false is a philosophic question of the kind "who is the best composer?" In the sense that there is no best composer, so the Marxist scheme is neither true nor false. To attack it as false is as foolish as to promote it as true—and both are equally useless in helping the educational development of a student who holds such a scheme to be true. To believe that these very general organizing schemes are true or false is an epistemological confusion characteristic of the philosophic stage.

The development of general schemes is a reflection of very abstract forms of thought becoming dominant in students' thinking. Abstract concepts begin to form and become increasingly general through the romantic stage. Much is made in educational literature of the beginnings of abstract conceptualization, largely due to Piaget's findings. This is clearly important, but *educationally*, it is just the relatively trivial first signs of a process that reaches fruition in the generation of the kinds of schemes I have been discussing in this chapter. When abstract thinking reaches the critical point of coalescence of romantic knowledge into philosophic general schemes, students make an important educational transition. This critical transition is virtually ignored in the literature on development, indicating yet again that education is not the focus of other developmental theories and that when we use them to think about educational issues, we may find our attention directed away from quite crucial educational phenomena.

The process of development into and through the philosophic stage is quite unlike the process suggested by an expanding horizons model. General schemes coalesce quite suddenly and provide a means for imposing an initial crude order on disparate elements. Only after a first crude order has been created is it possible to refine and clarify it. That is, one does not gradually build a superstructure after careful composition of the elements, rather one builds a superstructure first and then works on the elements within it.

Particularly at this philosophic stage, teaching requires a Christ-like sympathy for and sensitivity to those being taught—that they might have life and have it more abundantly. Abundance of life comes in part from assimilating to oneself, primarily through words, the richness of others' human experience and from informing our own experience with that richness. Despite many educational fashions that at present discount the importance of accumulating knowledge, ignorance of the world and its store of words remains the main enemy of education and one of the prominent causes of the poverty of individual experience.

# 4

# THE IRONIC STAGE

Approximate ages, 19/20
through adulthood

## CHARACTERISTICS
### From philosophic to ironic

During the philosophic stage students focus on abstract general schemes as the sources of truth. Progress through the philosophic stage is marked by an increasing sophistication of the schemes in response to accumulating knowledge. The transition from the philosophic to the ironic stage comes with students' appreciation that the general schemes cannot fully accommodate all the particulars and that no general scheme can adequately reflect the richness and complexity of reality.

Like other transitions between stages, this is a period of potential crisis. Though the ground has been gradually prepared for it during the philosophic stage, the transition happens quite quickly. The philosophic students' commitment, or connection, is to the truth, and transition out of the philosophic stage requires the recognition that what has been looked to as the source of truth is in fact empty. A successful transition to the ironic stage is achieved by preserving the commitment to truth, but recognizing that it is particulars that can be established as true, not the general schemes. Accepting this involves giving up their philosophic security and re-establishing, yet again, a new intellectual security. Perhaps even more than others, this transition requires intellectual courage. The danger is that the student will prefer the security offered by the general scheme and will dismiss everything that challenges it as meaningless or irrelevant.

A further difficulty in achieving a successful transition to the ironic stage is that at the same time as students recognize that the general schemes are not true, they find them, nevertheless, to be necessary. That is, even while students' location of secure truth is passing from general schemes to particular knowledge, they realize that unorganized particulars by themselves are meaningless. It is only when particulars form some pattern, are organized by some general scheme, that they become meaningful.

The resolution of this dilemma comes in the realization of the proper epistemological status of the general schemes. They are no longer perceived as either true or false, but are seen to be more or less useful—useful for organizing particulars into larger meaningful units. But is this not simply reverting to a philosophic imposition of meaning? No, quite the reverse. It is now the particulars that determine the general scheme, not the other way round.

At the philosophic stage, if particulars cannot be accommodated by a general scheme, if they remain anomalous, so much the worse for them—they are ignored, suppressed or considered irrelevant. At the ironic stage, if particulars cannot be accommodated by a general scheme, so much the worse for the general scheme—it is discarded and replaced by a scheme that can accommodate the particulars. As at the philosophic stage, so at the ironic stage meaning is composed by a dialectical interaction between general scheme and particular knowledge. Whereas it is characteristic of the philosophic stage that the general scheme is dominant, it is characteristic of the ironic stage that particular knowledge is dominant.

To return to the rough map metaphor used earlier: at the philosophic stage students impose an initial order on the world by laying a crude grid across it. This allows them to locate particular features by reference to the grid. Progress through the philosophic stage may be represented as filling in more and more detail between the grid lines and as refining the map in every respect. Transition to the ironic stage may be represented as locating the details by reference to each other.

This perception of truth in particularity also leads to an end of what I have been calling narcissism. Students' interest in the world is no longer determined by the requirements of their immature egos, and knowledge may be pursued, unfettered by the various constraints of immaturity, for its own sake. To signal the achievement of educational maturity which this stage represents, I will refer to the adult rather than the student from this point on, even though many ironic adults may well be officially students.

### Ironic stories

The world persists as it is, regardless of what we think about it. Our ideas, hypotheses, plots, schemes, patterns are products of our minds and do not affect the world's infinite particularity. The ironic mind is interested in the world's particularity for its own sake. It is interested in itself only as a part of the world's particularity and to understand in what ways the mind's methods of imposing order on, or making sense of, the world interferes with what is actually real and true about it.

I call this stage ironic because its key characteristic is a clear sense of what the mind contributes to knowledge. Put more gnomically, it represents a clear appreciation of where we end and the world begins. At the previous stages there is a kind of confusion, in which things that are a product of our modes of perception or manner of organizing knowledge are assumed to be a part of the world. This is exemplified at a simple level by young children assuming that the moon follows them along the street, or in a more complex way by the philosophic assumption that an ideology imposed on history is a part of historical reality, or more subtly yet, it is exemplified by our tendency to reify concepts we name and by the general bewitchment language spins around our perception and understanding.

The term *ironic stories* involves a kind of contradiction. I have been using *story* throughout the previous chapters to mean not simply once-upon-a-time fictions, but as a more pervasive form which we use in organizing knowledge. Mythic, romantic, and philosophic uses of the story form involve imposing more or less complex mental forms on knowledge about the world and involve a greater or lesser failure to distinguish the contribution made by the mind. In this sense, irony is the great dissolver of stories, the under-miner of plots and patterns. In its success in distinguishing the contribution made to knowledge by the mind, it dissolves and undermines the various confusions characteristic of the previous stages. And in its perception of the necessity, but not truth, of story forms it is liberating. That is, it allows the adult to select one or many schemes, or other story forms, to give best order and fullest meaning to the knowledge at hand.

The process we have been following may be characterized in a number of general ways, some of which I will consider in the conclusions. In as far as the story form represents an important method whereby the mind imposes order on phenomena, and this form becomes increasingly more sophisticated and less determining as we progress through the stages, we can suggest as one dimension of a general characterization of educational development that it is a process which begins with mental forms determining what is per-ceived of the world and ends with mental forms conforming to the complex particular reality of the world as far as they can. There are no stories or discontinuities in the world, they are created by our imposition of beginnings and ends.

As there are no stories at the ironic stage, or rather as everything may be embodied in various stories, so too there are no games, or everything may become part of a game. Escape from the *serious* games of the philosophic stage, frees the ironic mind to introduce the mythic, romantic, and philosophic senses of games and play into everything, guided by aesthetic criteria of appropriateness. Whereas at the philosophic stage life was reduced to, and imprisoned in, some game, at the ironic stage all the forms of play may infuse any activity and give life that quality of joyfulness or creative gaiety that Friedrich Nietzsche and William Butler Yeats have celebrated. Whereas at the philosophic stage an absolute separation was made between serious roles and recreation, people at the ironic stage tend not to distinguish at all clearly between work and play, between their careers and leisure. Indeed, the idea of certain activities being separated on grounds of seriousness and forming a career is quite alien to the ironic consciousness.

Irony is often perceived as merely playful, unserious, uncommitted. This seems to me a simple minded view. Rather, irony is prerequisite to full seriousness and sincerity. We cannot take at face value that overly earnest sincerity of the philosophic commitment to some ideological or metaphysical system. Only when that layer of (self-) deception has been pierced can one come to deal seriously with serious things and to be sincere, in the knowledge of just what sincerity entails. It is for this reason, I think, that James Joyce, one of the great ironists of this century, most admired in life and in art the qualities of sincerity and seriousness.[1]

## Leave nothing behind

The stages are not to be seen as stages we pass through and leave behind. Each stage contributes something vital and necessary to the mature adult's ability to make sense of the world and human experience. I will consider these contributions in more detail in chapter 6, but here I need to give some indication of these contributions in order to provide even a brief sketch of the characteristics of the ironic stage. That is, the ironic stage is made up of the accumulated contributions of the previous stages, all under the control of the key ironic perception outlined above.

What is contributed by the mythic stage? The child—who is indeed father of the man—learns to project his inner mental images

[1] See Richard Ellmann, "The Politics of Joyce," *The New York Review of Books,* June 9, 1977, pp. 41–46.

onto the world and so give human meaning to it. The mythic ability
to connect the mind to the world is fundamental to all later learning.
However sophisticated thinking may become and however well the
mythic level is controlled by irony, the establishment of meaning
requires the projection of mental forms onto the world and some
basic affective orientation toward whatever particular knowledge is
being dealt with. Though the adult may use many-termed systems to
organize knowledge, underlying these will be found those most
basic binary opposites on which later thinking is elaborated—
good/bad, fear/security, etc. The mythic stage contributes the ability to derive human meaning from the inhuman world.

The romantic stage contributes the ability to inhabit imaginatively other times, places, and forms of living. It contributes to the
adult a sense of vivacity, vitality, and bouyancy in dealing with the
world. It contributes, in short, a sense of romance. However well
irony keeps the adult's sense of romance in check, the ability to form
romantic associations with knowledge is necessary to give energy
and enthusiasm to learning. The lack of romance leads to either
ignorant dullness or knowledgeable pedantry.

The philosophic stage contributes the ability to search for the
recurrent, the typical, for laws and patterns. It contributes the ability
to organize knowledge into more generally meaningful schemes. If
at the philosophic stage these schemes tend to be out of control,
dominating knowledge and inquiry inappropriately, once controlled by an ironic intelligence they become flexible servants, enabling
the perception of a variety of ways of making sense of social, psychological, and historical processes, and of one's place and role as an
agent or participant in them.

To extend the rough metaphor used in chapter 2: whereas the
mythic stage was represented as a kind of cognitive recapitulation of
the Freudian primary process, and the romantic stage as a kind of
cognitive recapitulation of the secondary process, one may see the
ironic stage as a rough cognitive equivalent of the development of
the superego in the personality. It does not destroy or replace the
previously developed structures, rather it controls them and uses

them for more mature purposes. Similarly, the ironic intelligence controls and uses the contributions of the previous stages for its own mature purpose.

And what is this purpose? It is to be able to answer Pilate's ironic question, "What is truth?" in its own ironic way. And why should we want to do that? Knowing the truth, as John Keats observed, provides humans with an aesthetic pleasure—the kind of joy which Nietzsche and Yeats have written about most articulately—which both motivates and justifies the search.[2]

## TEACHING AND LEARNING
## AT THE IRONIC STAGE

If the learner is at the ironic stage, the ironic stage teacher does not have to organize knowledge in a manner different from the way the teacher understands it. Consequently I will not give examples of how the characteristics of this stage affect how knowledge should be organized for most effective learning.[3] Teaching at this stage is largely a matter of seeking the most economical ways of providing the learner with access to greater knowledge or expertise. It is a cooperative venture whose only unequality will be the teacher's greater knowledge, skill, or experience.

## CONCLUSION

Educational and moral development seem largely distinct processes, but there is a small area where they seem to overlap. Another dimension of the process we have been following here may be characterized as the move away from the self toward the world. The

[2] The characterization of this ironic stage could be enriched by adding much of Erikson's description of "ego integrity" and Lawrence Kohlberg's outline of his sixth stage of moral development.

[3] For a discussion of how one might teach history at the ironic stage see G. R. Elton, *The Practice of History* (Sydney: Sydney University Press, 1967).

achievement of the ironic stage is the opening up of the mystical insight, by forgetting our self, we finally find ourself. Ironic scholarship requires something that is a part of sanctity, the denial of the self and the full acceptance and acknowledgment of the autonomy and value of other—whether other people or other knowledge. In the previous stages, to revert to the example of history, past reality was made subservient to the ego's requirements; only at the ironic stage is one able to properly pursue and establish a truth uninfected by our ego's needs and independent of the self. The achievement and expression of such a truth are as rare as hen's teeth, of course. But people we consider great manage it, and such truth is the proper aim of educated people.

# 5

# SOME COMMENTS
# ON THE STAGES

The four stages of educational development have been distinguished from one another as clearly as possible, and it is now necessary to complicate the picture somewhat. What I have sketched so far is an ideal development from one pure stage to the next. Now I must infuse some of the murkiness of the real world and must consider some additional dimensions and implications of the stages.

### Leave nothing behind

First, to repeat a point made in the previous chapter, these stages should not be seen as phases we pass through and leave behind. If this were the case, we might consider them regrettable imperfections to be overcome as quickly as possible, moving the child directly to an ironic appreciation of the world. Unfortunately, this happens all too frequently. The educational ineffectiveness of this is rarely very evident, because children can learn almost anything and our typical means of evaluating learning are so crude that an ability to repeat things is accepted as evidence of adequate learning. All learning, however, is not equally valuable, and some learning is not *educationally* valuable at all. The crudest distinction we can make is between learning which remains, in Whitehead's sense, "inert", and that which, in Piaget's sense, serves as food, or an "aliment," to the process of educational development. The theory I am expressing in this book suggests that it is not particular knowledge that can be classified as "inert" or an "aliment," but rather it is the context, the way of organizing, of making accessible and assimilable knowledge that will determine whether that particular knowledge will serve as an educational aliment or remain educationally inert. Put simply, if the knowledge is organized appropriately for the stage a student is at, it will serve as an aliment; if it is organized in a manner appropriate to a higher stage, it will remain inert.[1]

Attempting to hurry children to more mature stages has the bad effect of providing inadequate fulfillment of earlier stages. Inadequate satisfaction of the needs and interests of, say, the romantic stage will result in a deficiency in both the philosophic and ironic stages. That is, inadequate satisfaction of any stage leads to educational deficiences in the adult.[2] This leads to the simple principle that the fullest satisfaction of children's and students' needs and interests is the best preparation for their future as educated adults. John Dewey's emphasis on the importance of present experience in school for its own sake, rather than seeing it as solely preparation for

---

[1] This may seem to involve a claim similar to Jerome Bruner's celebrated dictum: "any subject can be taught effectively in some intellectually honest form to any child at any stage of development." My exploration of structure, however, focuses primarily on the child's forms of understanding, rather than on the structural characteristics of subject matter. That is, while I might want to qualify Bruner's claim somewhat, I generally agree with it, but I also presuppose it. I am trying rather to discover from a study of the child's changing modes of making sense of the world just what particular structures should be used at what stages for most effective learning. This is, of course, a task Bruner has also dealt with in his *Toward a Theory of Instruction* (Cambridge, Mass.: The Belknap Press of Harvard University Press, 1966). His stages—enactive, iconic, symbolic—deal with young children only, however, and his focus is largely psychological, not educational and is very strongly influenced by Piaget's stages.

[2] We are all educationally deficient in one way or another, of course. This theory does, however, provide some ways in which we might be able to diagnose more clearly the causes of certain deficiencies.

future life, has led to a mischievous dichotomy in some people's minds. Polemical debate has raged about whether schooling should be conceived as primarily preparation for the future, in which present satisfactions have to be sacrificed to supposed future benefits, or whether the present activities in schools must justify themselves as engaging on their own terms. This theory of educational development suggests that this is an unreal dichotomy and an idle debate. Proper fulfillment of the particular interests students have at any stage is the proper means of preparing them for the future (which, after all, only echoes what Dewey said in the first place).

Educational development is a cumulative process. The proper fulfillment and satisfaction of one stage leads on to the next, and subsequent stages build on, elaborate, and develop from the previous ones, gathering their benefits and enriching perception and the sense made of the world and human experience. Ideally we should leave nothing behind; a properly educated adult should still be able to see the world with the eyes of a child.

### Partial satisfaction of stages

The relatively straightforward picture of distinct stages presented in the previous four chapters becomes a little more complicated if one sees the ironic stage as encompassing the philosophic, romantic, and mythic; the philosophic encompassing the romantic and mythic; and the romantic encompassing the mythic. We must complicate this picture a little further now by considering how we may, within the same minute, engage one topic at, say, a romantic level and another at, say, an ironic level. Still further complication must be added by considering implications of the fact that typically full satisfaction of a stage is not necessary before developing some characteristics of the next stage.

For this theory to be useful, let alone sensible, it must be able to account for the complexity and variety of forms of educational development that anyone can observe from even the most casual contact with those around them. So far this theory can only account for four general categories. The temptation at this point is to dwell on the complications inherent in the theory to show how it can account for a very wide range of different forms of educational development, and, thus, in the process, to drown the simple underlying theory in qualifications. I will try to resist this temptation by restricting the discussion of complications to the point where the theory's ability to indeed account for a much wider range of forms of educational development is clearly indicated—I will not try to give exhaustive descriptions.

The stages should not be seen as monolithic, in the way that might be encouraged by the initial characterizations in the previous chapters. With the exception of the mythic stage, a person cannot be thought of as being exclusively in any particular stage. Typically, the student who predominately makes sense of things in a romantic way, will also be amenable to seeing things in a mythic way. As one progresses through the stages, one remains open to the appeal, and manner of seeing, of all the previous stages. When engaging something in a manner appropriate to a stage prior to our best achievement, we tend to consider it as less than fully *serious,* as something appealing to less than our best intelligence, as recreation or entertainment. This is not lost on Hollywood, of course. Unresistingly, we accept stories that pit absolute good against absolute bad, though our best intelligence knows that such conflicts are simplistic. We are, as it were, quite ready to pretend away the accumulated elaborations and sophistications and derive pleasure and meaning from more simple ways of seeing.

We always retain the ability to be engaged by knowledge organized in a manner appropriate to a previous stage. An adult at the ironic stage has the ability to flit casually through these various ways of organizing knowledge, engaging a single topic in each mode, flexibly deriving fullest and richest meaning from it. This suggests the not altogether absurd parody; after a good night's sleep, one may in the morning be predominately at the ironic stage; by afternoon be philosophic; by early evening, romantic; and by night, mythic. It seems to be true that as we grow tired we find it difficult to sustain the kind of intellectual energy required for working at our best level. For some kinds of work this is no bad thing. Some writers seem to do their best creative work at night, with alcohol in their blood. This seems to release the control of ironic consciousness and give freer reign to myth and romance. A not uncommon method of work is to write wild at night and revise cold in the ironic morning.

Another complication: some people seem able to reach, say, a philosophic stage when engaging a particular topic or kind of work, but engage nearly everything else at a lower level. The general tendency, however, is for a philosophic appreciation of one topic to exert a pressure to organize everything else philosophically. If someone has developed a strong ideology, the tendency is for it to absorb everything else. But one observes exceptions, for example, the wild ideologue, ready to destroy civilizations for his idea, who never gets over his passion for collecting early Victorian postage stamps or breeding Siamese cats.

Connected to the above observations is a more general sense in which progress through the stages rarely follows the ideal path sketched in the first four chapters—an image of a person fully developing each stage, then moving smoothly on to the next, to achieve a rich and mature ironic appreciation of things. This process was fed at each stage by knowledge precisely organized in a manner that best promoted progress through each stage and into the next. In reality a typical child faces a variety of sources of knowledge, few if any of which are sensitive to how knowledge should be organized to be most meaningful and useful to the child; television, adults' conversations, a variety of teachers at various stages of educational development, other children's conversations, newspapers, hobbies, books, and so on. What effect does this have on the smooth picture presented earlier?

To help answer this question I need to state one of the stronger claims I wish to make about these stages; a claim I will discuss later in this chapter. That is, the process of educational development I have described earlier is a *natural* process: the sequence of stages I have sketched is a *necessary* sequence. No one can reach the ironic stage without first passing through the mythic, romantic, and philosophic stages. This is because the earlier stages contribute things that are prerequisite to the later stages. In that the ironic stage is partially constituted of those accumulated residues of the mythic, romantic, and philosophic stages sketched in the previous chapter, it follows that an ironic understanding cannot be achieved except by passing through the previous stages.

I will discuss this claim later, but here I need to add a major qualification to it: the capacities of each stage do not need to be fully developed before a later stage's manner of organizing knowledge can become meaningful. That is, partial satisfaction of a stage, partial development of the capacities of a stage, can supply sufficient pre-requisites for engagement with the following stage. To return to a previous example: if a student is just beginning to develop romantic associations with historical characters or events, our Marxist teacher at the philosophic stage may well persuade the student that such associations are childish and a degenerate bourgeois fantasy, and introduce the student to the unfolding dialectical process of history. What will likely result? The natural pressure to go through the stages sequentially may interfere with the teacher's purposes in two ways. First, the knowledge of the dialectical unfolding of history by class struggle may be learned but remain largely inert, (possibly becoming an aliment later when the student is ready to move to the philosophic stage); second, the student may more subtley, unin-tentionally, and undetectedly subvert the teacher's purpose by sim-ply developing a romantic association with the laws of history, with the Marxist dialectic, which becomes, in effect, the student's hero. This kind of romantic pseudo-philosophic approach to his-tory is not so uncommon, even among historians. If the teacher is successful, however, and gets the student to see history in a philo-sophic way, the likely result would be a philosophic appreciation that is largely deficient in those capacities that should ideally have been contributed during the romantic stage. That is, such a philo-sophic appreciation of history would be deficient in an imaginative and sympathetic sense of the past as a record of the lives of flesh and blood people both similar to and different from ourselves; it would be a sense of the past possessed by the kind of desiccated ideologue to whom history is open mainly to calculation and not to under-standing.

My claim, however, is that it is only after students have made *some* progress into the romantic stage that it becomes possible for them to understand and use knowledge organized in a philosophic way. It would not, then, be possible to introduce a child at the mythic stage to a meaningful philosophic perspective on history. Any learning the mythic student might display would of necessity be inert (though possibly becoming an aliment later, if remembered). A philosophic appreciation of history requires, for example—in however attenuated a form—those capacities I have characterized as a sense of otherness. Those capacities are not developed in any usable form until the romantic stage.

If *some* development of the capacities of a stage are necessary before one can begin to have access to the next, two questions arise: what is the minimum development that will nevertheless allow progress through the stages, and what is the result of only partial development of the capacities of particular stages? This is not something one can quantify precisely, but it will help to clarify the following points if I use numbers. These should not be read as precise statistics, because they are not. Rather they should be read as metaphors and should be interpreted quite loosely.

By metaphoric quantification, then, I will suggest some basic principles relevant to the questions above. Development of 25% of the capacities of a stage are prerequisite to the development of any of the capacities of the next stage. Development of only 25% of the capacities of one stage would permit the development of only 5% of the capacities of the next stage and nothing of the stage after that. Development of 75% of the capacities of one stage would permit the development of 55% of the capacities of the next stage and 30% of the capacities of the stage after that. Development of 100% of the capacities of one stage would permit the development of 100% of all further stages—this is the ideal sketched in the first four chapters. If one hopes to reach the ironic stage, at least 80% of the capacities of the mythic stage, 65% of the romantic stage, 50% of the philosophic will need to be developed.

This might seem like educational statistics gone mad—or it would if one did not see this kind of quantification occasionally taken quite literally. Here, however, I mean these numbers just as an economical way of articulating some complications about the stages.

To elaborate on the first quantification: if one developed only 25% of the capacities of the romantic stage, then one could hope to develop no more than 5% of those of the philosophic stage. That is, one might have some access to the philosophic manner of organizing knowledge, but sustained thinking using philosophic capacities is greatly restricted. But what about our desiccated ideologues? Are they perhaps not an example of, say, 25% development of the capacities of the romantic stage, and 50% of those of the philosophic? I am unsure whether or not this is possible. It seems to me that the tendency is always to a decreasing ability to develop the capacities of later stages, once those of an earlier stage have been scanted. Desiccated ideologues seem much more likely to have enormously overdeveloped the 5% of the philosophic stage to which they have access, leading to a very imbalanced and narrow perspective.

One could go on at great length discussing the characteristics of people who had developed various permutations of the capacities of the different stages—80% mythic, 30% romantic, 10% philosophic; 40% mythic, 10% romantic; and so on. Silly as these numbers may seem if taken literally, when read as metaphors they indicate that it is the principle of the partial development of the capacities of the different stages that enables this theory to account for the vast variety of forms of educational development we may see from casual observation. The capacities not developed or only partially developed will lead to particular deficiencies. It should be possible eventually to map out just what deficiencies result from inadequate development of what capacities. I will begin this in a preliminary way in the next chapter.

One fairly obvious principle articulated by means of the numbers above is the importance of the earlier stages. Minimal development of the capacities of the mythic stage will stunt further educational development. It follows that our best efforts should go to promoting the fullest development of the mythic capacities of young children.

Even if one has begun developing the capacities of a higher

stage can one not continue to develop those of a lower stage at the same time or later? Cannot a person who has achieved minimal access to the philosophic stage continue to develop romantic capacities, which in turn will help the further development of philosophic capacities? This may be possible to some degree, but it seems that entry to a higher stage inhibits further development at lower stages. It is as though the process allows only a single, or predominant, growth point, and this is always at the most advanced point one has reached. Going back and firming up the foundations after one has begun building seems extremely difficult.

This may help to explain why, despite learning things every day throughout their lives, people's educational development stops, and stops so frequently at the earlier stages. (I think it is not an unfair estimate that about 80% of the populations of western countries develop only minimally beyond the romantic stage. Most popular magazines and television programs are directed at mythic and romantic levels.) It is not traumas that stop people's educational development, rather it is more like a withering. As with a plant that withers, we might more often look for the cause to the root rather than the leaves or flowers. Inadequate development of the capacities of the mythic stage prevents much further development. This, of course, does not deprive such people of pleasure from entertaining knowledge, or make them any less valuable as human beings, or necessarily stunt their moral, or social, or psychological development.

What are the causes of inadequate development at the mythic stage? Bad teaching, stupid curricula and school activities, of course, may be major contributors. But probably more frequently it follows on inadequate stimulation as a baby, an impoverished linguistic environment, a lack of the love that begins to open us to the world. One of the most depressing results of much study of development is the conclusion that if the initial stages of a baby's development have been scanted in some way, one is more or less helpless to rectify the situation later. This theory suggests a similar brutal point about educational development: if the earliest stages are scanted, there is little hope for much progress to more advanced stages.

But, having said all this, it is necessary to stress that we are resilient creatures. I am trying here to describe what I observe, and, no doubt as with most readers, I would like to believe I am wrong. We do observe cases where these general rules seem to be contravened, and, in those exceptions, lies the hope that we *can* recuperate early losses. The evidence that suggests we cannot is far from compelling and has been powerfully argued against recently.[3] But our major effort should be to discover what is true, not to promote what we would like to believe.

Knowledge that serves as an aliment to the process of educational development may provide an aesthetic pleasure. Similarly knowledge organized in a form assimilable at a level below that of one's highest achievement may be entertaining. Such entertaining knowledge seems to be neither an aliment to the process of development at the higher stage of development, nor an aliment to the fuller development of the lower stage. If someone is at the philosophic stage, for example, romantic knowledge will not be an aliment to development through the philosophic stage, but neither will it be an aliment to further romantic development. It will be simply entertaining, of interest and value for the pleasure it provides, but, as with inert knowledge, it will not contribute to educational development. So we may call knowledge organized in a manner appropriate to a stage in advance of one's best achievement, *inert;* knowledge organized in a manner appropriate to a stage lower than one's best achievement, *entertaining*; and knowledge organized in a manner appropriate to the stage of one's best achievement, an *aliment* to further development.

If it is indeed true that achieving, say, the philosophic stage inhibits to a greater or lesser degree further development of the capacities of the romantic stage, then this provides a strong argument against trying to hurry someone through the stages. It leads to the principle that the capacities of any stage should be developed as fully as possible before encouraging transition to the next.

[3] See A. M. and A.D.B. Clarke, *Early Experience: Myth and Evidence,* The Developing Child, eds. Jerome Bruner, Michael Cole, and Barbara Lloyd (London: Open Books, 1977).

Intelligence and educational
development

What relationship do these stages have to intelligence? Are people with low intelligence restricted or prevented from developing through these stages, and can only people with high intelligence progress smoothly through them? Intelligence is an elusive notion (and IQ seems to me a quite bizarre one). To ask whether people with low intelligence are inhibited from developing through the stages suggests a notion of intelligence that is independent of educational development. It smacks of the notion of some kind of innate intelligence that is high or low and that determines an individual's success or failure in achieving educational development.

Our genetic makeup leads to the development of certain traits within the context of environments that provide appropriate aliments. To take a crude example: during our early teens, our genetic structure, given appropriate environmental supports, normally leads to those physical developments we characterize as puberty. If a child is given no food after the first year of life, to starkly make the point, that child will not reach puberty. Genetic structure cannot determine a trait independently of particular environmental conditions. Similarly, it makes no sense to posit an innate intelligence that *determines* later intellectual achievements independently of particular environmental conditions.

If a child is given a diet with particular deficiencies, puberty may be delayed. Varied diets will lead to slightly different physical developments. If a child's educational environment is deficient in the aliments appropriate to the romantic stage, that child will have difficulty developing through that stage. Depending on environmental aliments, the character of a particular individual's development will vary. Adequate development through the stages, then, will most sensibly be seen not as being *the result of* high intelligence, but *as* high intelligence. Intelligence in any sensible usage is made up of a variety of capacities; the development of the capacities constituent of intelligence is integral to the process of educational development. Any problems with early adaptations, or inadequate access to the aliments that support development through a stage, will show up as intellectual deficiencies.

This might seem opaque in the current climate of education, where a single number IQ score is thought by many people not only to tell something educationally important about a person, but to be a measure of some innate quality. Given the model of educational development used here, intelligence that is somehow independent of environmental aliments does not make sense. It does not make sense to say that people with low intelligence cannot develop far through the stages; rather, one might say that the interaction of gene functioning and environmental aliments was in some way inadequate in developing the capacities of, say, the mythic stage—this lack of achievement is low intelligence.

But, given similar environments, will not some people develop certain capacities better than others because genetically they are more sensitive to the appropriate environmental aliments, and so their achieved intelligence will be to some extent due to their genetic endowment? And if this is so, does it not make sense to try to measure what proportion of achieved intelligence is normally due to these genetic differences? Surely, yes, to both the above questions. But, it is false to suppose that in providing some measure of the genetic contribution to achieved intelligence that one is measuring innate intelligence. One is measuring sensitivity to particular kinds of environmental aliments. In that individual sensitivity will likely vary from aliment to aliment, and the concept of critical period will provide a crucial variable because an individual's sensitivity to particular aliments will wax and wane, what is to be measured is enormously complicated. And it is clear that the kinds of crude measures one gets from, say, comparing identical twins reared in different environments tell us very little about this.

Is this merely a quibble? Am I simply substituting "genetic sensitivity to certain aliments" for "innate intelligence"? Yes, but this is more than a quibble. It is to substitute an interactive for a static concept. I do not want to deny that genetic differences affect later intelligence, nor the likelihood that we can provide some kind of measures of the contribution of genetic difference to intelligence.

I want to stress, however, that intelligence is a meaningful concept *only within* a specific cultural context, and that genetic sensitivity to certain aliments is not innate intelligence, given any sensible use of the term intelligence. Intelligence involves the use of certain capacities; genetic sensitivity to certain aliments may lead to the development of those capacities given an environment rich in the appropriate aliments.

Such a notion of intelligence does not, of course, obviate the possibility of providing measures of it. One could provide measures of a number of the specifiable capacities that comprise such a notion of intelligence. This would give something like the profiles of educational achievement or skill attainment that are now quite common. One result of such a notion, however, is that it does resist mindless single-number attribution to some mythical innate intelligence.

The question of whether these stages of educational development are universally valid is a product of a similar confusion. The categories and characteristics that I have sketched are the result of a particular culture evoking, encouraging, and sustaining genetic unfolding in this particular form. That is, they are natural only within this culture, but within this culture, I am claiming, they *are* natural: they represent approximately the ideal form of educational development whereby this culture develops the largest range of capacities.

The question of whether it is possible to devise culturally unbiased measurements of intelligence is similarly confused. This is not an empirical question to be settled by an ingenious composer of test items. Given the interactive notion of the growth of intelligence outlined above, it is logically impossible to provide such measurements. Cultures are not only different because they offer different environmental aliments. They are more profoundly different because different aliments evoke, stimulate, and encourage a different set of the vast range of human sensitivities which, in continuing interaction with the aliments, lead to the development of more or less different capacities. Which is to say, one cannot create a culturally unbiased measurement of intelligence simply by neutralizing environmental differences. It has been assumed that once that task has been performed then one may directly measure capacities common to all cultures. It is not just the environmental differences that distinguish one cultural group from another, but also the capacities that different cultures develop. That is, there is no norm of human nature independent of culture which may form a base or standard for culturally unbiased measurement. Man is a cultural animal; culture is a part of our nature.

The confusion inherent in these questions follows from the false assumption that genes determine certain traits, that there is some ideal form toward which genetic unfolding will lead. An ideal form can be meaningful only by reference to the specific environment in which the individual exists.

## Simplification and falsification

Educational development does not proceed by gradual accumulation of knowledge and understanding. It goes by fits and starts, by stages which involve quite sudden shifts of focus and kinds of understanding. It does not gradually build orderly pictures of the world; it begins with crude general pictures which are then elaborated, refined, and qualified. My attempts to identify the main characteristics of children's thinking at that level of generality most appropriate for education's concerns has led me to suggest that knowledge be organized to complement those characteristics, and this has led to some unfashionable recommendations. I have suggested that history be simplified for the mythic stage to the point of being a kind of fairy story where light struggles for survival against wicked darkness; to the point where for the romantic stage principles of selection be applied which turn history into a set of transcendent events and characters; to the point for the philosophic stage where history is reduced to ideologies and metaphysical systems. My examples are full of such simplifications, which may seem to many readers to amount to falsifications. I want at this point to defend the appropriateness of more or less greatly simplifying historical as well as other kinds of content.

My examples all seem to involve taking sides, seeing things as good or bad without much neutrality in between. This manner of dealing with history disturbs some people. The example of personifying countries gave us, "England was greedy and wanted to become richer, so it conquered people all over the world and forced them to buy English goods." All very well, old boy, but hardly the whole story—my millions of English stockbroker readers may respond. Indeed, not the whole story. One could, however, select particulars from historical reality that would support such a generalization. Such a selection would be biased—comes the response. Well, yes. But so is every attempt to represent historical reality in a narrative. Words are different stuff from reality; the latter does not conveniently allow itself to be transmuted into the former. The attempt to better reflect reality in words is of course the struggle of all scholars.

But even if simplification and selection are necessary for even the most sophisticated historiography, are not my examples so biased as to be considered false? The more general a statement, the more difficult it is to show that it is false. Even something that seems on the face of it false, say, "Tyrants are good," may be so general that it cannot be shown to be false. It might be defended on the line of argument that we owe most to those historical characters we like least. Unless we introduce untrue particulars, it is hard to show that any very general or simplified account is actually false. Certainly one cannot show that the claim about England's greed is *false*. One *can* show that it is inadequate to account for all kinds of particulars that are a part of historical reality. This is the process mentioned earlier of qualifying, refining, and elaborating.

Similarly other simplifications involved in my examples—that civilization is good and things that hinder it are bad—cannot be shown to be *false*. They are simply inadequate to account for all the phenomena from which such generalizations are derived.

I am not writing here, even if I could, a philosophical treatise on history. I want only to point out that the process of educational development is one in which access to knowledge is achieved in particular ways, and, in teaching, we must take account of these ways. Initial access to knowledge, to understanding, to *meaning* at each stage is necessarily relatively crude, but elaboration, refinement, and qualification follow. If the initial relatively crude access is not achieved, elaboration, refinement, and qualification cannot follow. Certain stages and their forms of understanding do not simply precede, but are logically prerequisite to later stages and more sophisticated forms. Trying to skip the prerequisites because they are immature in one way or another is bizarre.

Analogous to the way very young children learn conceptual mastery of the temperature continuum—learning first hot and cold, then mediating these until they have developed a more or less elaborate set of concepts about temperature—is the way young children begin to make sense of historical phenomena. It is appropriate that they should use very general affective orienters like "good" and "bad," first because such terms are required to make the phenomena referred to meaningful, and also because it is only after *some* general organization has been achieved that the process of refinement, elaboration, and qualification can get underway. Such crude orienters as "good" and "bad," however, are only elaborated on, they are not overcome or left behind. Though they will not show so crudely, they will persist in even the most advanced scholarship.

Too often teachers avoid providing these relatively crude means of access to knowledge because of inappropriate scruples born of insecurity. As people are quite commonly taught to be ashamed of sentimentality and so never learn to exercise and control their sentiments, so people are taught to be ashamed of unsophisticated forms of historical and other understanding, and they never exercise and learn to control the prerequisites of mature historical understanding. The inability of so many teachers to feel comfortable with simpler forms of understanding and their modes of selection also derives from insecurity. The too frequent result is to undermine children's educational development either by presenting a kind of history that is largely meaningless to them or by concentrating on safe trivia that does not raise these awkward concerns.

## The necessity of teaching

Isaac Newton humbly pointed out that if he was able to see far it was because he was standing on the shoulders of giants. So, too, anyone who makes educational progress, who learns to make better sense of the world and experience, owes a debt of gratitude to those giants who first created the knowledge and fashioned the insights that we may gather in their wake. The stages I have sketched above seem to reflect something of the way in which individuals' intellectual development recapitulates that of the historical intellectual development of western culture.[4] The teacher's job, then, is to help children in a few years to gather to themselves the achievements whose first accomplishment took centuries and millenia. This has become a commonplace observation, but some of its implications for the necessity of sensitive teaching seem to be ignored by many educators.

In terms of the theory being expressed in this book, the best means of promoting educational development is by being sensitive to the stage of a person's highest achievement and organizing the knowledge to be learned in a manner appropriate to that stage, so that it both fulfills the needs of that stage and in so doing provides an aliment to further development. If the teacher is at the romantic stage and the student is at the philosophic stage, the teacher of necessity lacks the ability to organize knowledge so that it will serve as an aliment to the student's educational development. The romantic teacher may well be able to organize knowledge so that it is entertaining[5] for the philosophic student, but such learning will not promote educational development.

If one sees educational development in part as a process whereby individuals recapitulate the developmental process of their cul-

[4] For an argument that history writing has gone through stages of development very similar to those sketched earlier see Kieran Egan, "Progress in Historiography," *Clio*, fall, 1978.

[5] I perhaps need to stress that I do not mean this pejoritively. There is nothing wrong with being entertained while one learns. I am using this term, however, to distinguish learning which may give pleasure from learning which, in addition to giving pleasure also promotes educational development.

ture, the teacher ideally needs to be aware of that process, in both its historical and individual dimensions. Such awareness can exist only in people who have achieved a rich ironic understanding, and so it follows that, ideally, teachers should be at the ironic stage. Teachers who are at, say, the romantic stage will of necessity lack any overview of the process of educational development, and consequently will be unable to make a distinction between learning that will serve as an aliment to students' development and learning that is entertaining.

Learning that is entertaining usually provides an uncomplicated pleasure and is generally easily accessible to students. Learning that serves as an aliment also properly provides an aesthetic pleasure, but one that is more complicated. Such learning requires the expenditure of intellectual energy, has to overcome resistance, and requires continual intellectual courage. Learning that expands awareness and calls on these qualities yields this more complex pleasure. Such learning is difficult enough with the best of teaching; with inadequate teaching, students' only hope of educational development is to make for themselves the achievements that took millenia of indefatigable intellectual energy and genius. This is not to be expected. The cost of inadequate teaching, then, is students' inability to make *educational* progress; they will likely spend their time on entertaining learning.

This yields the not surprising principle that the educational development of students requires good teaching. This analysis, however, allows us to be a little more precise about both some of the features of good teaching and the requirement that teachers be at the very least one stage of educational development in advance of those they teach, and preferably have developed a large proportion of the capacities of the ironic stage. In reality, of course, no student is dependant upon one teacher. And with typical modern access to a variety of media, students will likely always have available some sources that will convey knowledge in a manner that will enable them to use it as an aliment. One problem with this undirected and more or less random access to knowledge is that it is educationally chaotic; a student may be extended prematurely to making sense of things at a higher stage before many of the capacities of a lower stage have been developed.

The role of the teacher suggested by this theory is very demanding. It requires sensitivity to the student's stage of educational development, the ability to organize knowledge so that it fulfills the requirements of that stage, encourages development of its capacities, and serves as an aliment to further development. It requires that the teacher be well advanced in the ironic stage, a prerequisite for which is substantial development of the capacities of all the previous stages.

It is common today to depreciate the role of teaching in the educational process. Much more emphasis tends to be placed on the activities of students' learning, in light of which teaching tends to be considered a rather passive, facilitative, fall-back function. This theory suggests that teaching should be a much more active, directive, and important function in the educational process. It suggests that simply leaving students open to the variety of sources of knowledge and leaving them to direct their own inquiry and learning, without carefully structuring the context which will determine the kind of meaning derived from knowledge, is to risk doing as much harm as good. I know this may seem reactionary, and is unfashionable. I am not, however, arguing for an authoritarian teacher who is constantly giving directions. I mean, rather, that—using whatever techniques, methods, media, approaches the teacher wishes—the irreducible requirement for good teaching suggested by this theory is that the teacher needs to impose an organization on knowledge that will ensure it best feeds the educational development of the young. The kinds of organization are those discussed in the first four chapters.

## Naturalistic and other fallacies

I have throughout mentioned the proper process of education, and above claimed that the stages I have sketched represent a natural sequence of educational development. Even if it is granted that I have accurately described the sequence by which children typically come to a mature understanding of the world and experience, why should this be considered the proper process, a natural process, or even a good process? Why should the capacities of the ironic stage represent highest educational achievements—what if someone values those of the mythic stage more highly?

To paraphrase G. K. Chesterton's response to whether the *Rubiayat* was improved in Edward Fitzgerald's translation from the Persian; these are questions I should not deal with here, and could not deal with anywhere. They raise enormously complicated issues beyond the scope of this book, but a few observations about them seem appropriate and may mitigate some of their force as objections to my theory.

What will survive the above objections is my claim that if you want to produce from your educational system people with the capacities I have characterized as belonging to the ironic stage and with the entailed accumulation of capacities from the mythic, romantic, and philosophic stages, you will have to go about it more or less the way I have prescribed. *That* claim will ultimately stand or fall or be revised on empirical grounds.

Human beings by nature have the ability to create and live in an undetermined variety of forms of culture; what the limits of that ability are is a question that fascinates anthropologists. Particular cultures actualize different human capacities in different combinations, more or less valuing particular skills, modes of thinking, forms of relationships, and so on. What I have tried to describe—or prescribe—in this book is the best way in which, due to the historically determined character of, what I will call for economy's sake, western culture, children can actualize those of their capacities that are most useful for survival and success within this culture.

This acknowledges that the theory is culture-bound. My line of defence for its value shifts now to pointing out that limiting its usefulness to western culture still allows it, if accurate, considerable significance. My defence for calling it natural despite acknowledging that it is culture-bound will follow below.

If the process I have described is in part an individual recapitulation of the development of western culture, the best education is the one which allows the fullest recapitulation of the culture's development. Given the existence of this culture and its history and the birth of children within it, their education must enable them to reconstruct the history of the culture in microcosm within themselves if they are going to be able to make sense of the world around them and their own experience. Like the water fish swim in, our culture is the context in which we live; it is the means we have to make the world and experience meaningful. The fullest meaning comes only from the fullest reconstruction of the culture.

In that any culture does not permit development of all human capacities, any particular culture can be seen as constraining. If one does not like the constraints of western culture one cannot get away from them by remaining ignorant of the culture. One can escape such constraints only "through the top," as it were, by extending that culture. To be able to do that requires first the fullest absorption of that culture. We most completely remain prisoners of a culture, as of a language, when we have only imperfect knowledge of it. Freedom comes only from mastery. Freedom from the constraints of western culture, then, comes from the fullest educational development, in the same way as great artistic and literary works come from the fullest disciplined control of the medium. If one does not much *like* western culture, the very capacity to not like it and to be critical of it is due to having been through the process of western educational development that actualizes the capacities of skepticism and criticism. Few other cultures offer their members the luxury of not liking them, or of actualizing the capacity to reflect critically on them. So, if my description is accurate, the question of whether or not the process described is *good* or not is an idle question. If one wants to be able to make sense of the world and experience in this culture the process is necessary. That is, within this historically determined culture, the process is natural. The interaction of human nature with this culture will lead, if the human is to fully master the forms of thought, perception, and expression of the culture, to their going through mythic, romantic, philosophic, and ironic stages.

Now that may not seem to take us very far, as it is all conditional upon the individual's educational process recapitulating the culture's development and the description being accurate; those are the more fundamental questions. What the above discussion is intended to indicate is only that, if the process *is* described accurately, it cannot be casually dismissed on the grounds that one does not like this culture, or that one values mythic capacities above ironic, or that one can achieve educational maturity more directly by some different route. We are the products of our history in more senses than one.

# 6

# SENSITIVE PERIODS
# AND CONTENT

### Critical periods

One of the areas of research of most potential value to education is the study of what have come to be known as *critical periods,* or, the term that seems to me preferable in discussing children's development, *sensitive periods.* The former term derives from studies of animal behavior, particularly Konrad Lorenz's work with goslings. Lorenz showed that there was a brief period, which occured within about a day of the goslings' births, during which it "imprinted" or fixed upon certain kinds of moving objects as a mother figure. In nature, the object that the gosling would have available when this capacity developed would be the real mother. By removing the gosling from its real mother, and exposing it, during the period when this capacity developed, to a clay model or to a human being, it was found that the gosling fixed on these as its mother instead. It would then treat the model or human as its mother for the rest of its life, following them in preference to its real mother when she was introduced after the critical period for mother-imprinting has passed.[1]

Whatever the survival value of this phenomenon, it exemplifies in a dramatic way that certain organisms are structured such that in their developmental process certain capacities unfold at certain periods. For development to proceed optimally it is necessary that the organism's environment provides the objects that will serve as best aliments at the appropriate periods. For the optimal development of the gosling, its environment should, and normally would, provide its mother during the critical period for imprinting its mother figure. Another way of putting this is to say that organisms have innate mechanisms that are preprogrammed to respond selectively to a particular range of stimuli within a certain time period in the organisms' life span. For optimal development the appropriate range of stimuli should be available at the appropriate period.

Can we identify such sensitive periods in human development? Or, if we cannot identify things quite as dramatic as the gosling's mother imprinting, can we identify periods during which certain kinds of things are best learned? Or, another way of putting the question, can we identify sensitive periods before or after which certain things cannot be learned, or can be learned only with increasing difficulty and inefficiency the further in time from the critical period? Clearly, if we could identify such sensitive periods, we could design a much more sensible curriculum.

Observation indicates a fairly dramatic sensitive period for developing the language capacity. If a child is deprived of a language-using environment, or is exposed to an impoverished linguistic environment, between the ages of roughly one and four years then, in the case of extreme deprivation, the child will find it difficult if not impossible to become an effective language user. The degree of deprivation or impoverishment seems to correlate highly with how fluent or otherwise a language user the child becomes.

[1] See Konrad Lorenz, *The Comparative Method of Studying Innate Behavior Patterns*, Symposium of the Society for Experimental Biology, vol. 4 (New York: Academic Press, 1950); and Konrad Lorenz, *Evolution and Modification of Behavior* (Chicago: University of Chicago Press, 1956).

Empirical research is exposing other clear cases of sensitive periods in humans. The first months of life seem to be a sensitive period for the perception and discrimination of forms. This capacity may be most efficiently developed during this sensitive period. If babies are kept in dull environments that lack the appropriate stimuli that will best encourage development of this capacity during this period, it seems that later the capacity to perceive and discriminate forms undergoes relatively little further development. As the capacity to read depends on the capacity to make relatively fine and rapid discriminations of forms, this early sensitive period is obviously very important for all later educational development. Many children's inability to read, or their functional illiteracy, seems to be due to their inability to distinguish the forms of letters clearly and rapidly. No amount of practise during late elementary or secondary school years seems able to develop this capacity to the extent that such children become really fluent readers. The fact seems to be, surprisingly, that the sensitive period for developing this prerequisite for reading seems to come to a close within the first year of life.

The capacity to read also seems to have its sensitive period.[2] Contrary to present popular belief and the conveniences of our school systems, and disasterously out of step with current practice, the sensitive period for learning to read seems to be largely coincident with, and logically connected to, the sensitive period for acquiring a first language—that is, between the ages of two and five years.[3]

Genetic biology is suggesting with increasing persuasiveness that the developmental process involves a *continuum* from what we more readily recognize as biological adaptation (like form perception) to what we consider educational learning (like learning to read

[2] See W. Ragan Callaway, Jr., *Modes of Biological Adaptation and Their Role in Intellectual Development*, Perceptual Cognitive Development Monographs, vol. 1, no. 1 (The Galton Institute, 1970).

[3] Among its other achievements, *Sesame Street*, the U.S. television series produced by the Children's Television Workshop, has shown that it is possible to teach elementary reading to large numbers of children by age three, with relatively infrequent instruction.

or learning about the history of Ireland). The earlier adaptations are more amenable to precise study, but later changes in interest and ability to deal with different kinds of learning may be more sensibly studied if we see them in the terms suggested by genetic biology. If the proactive role of gene function ensures that we respond selectively to particular ranges of stimuli within certain time intervals during our life spans, we might sensibly consider generally observable changes in our focus of interest, not as casual shifts, but rather as sensitive periods during which we are especially amenable to particular kinds of learning.

How, then, might we go about identifying the main sensitive periods in educational development? We are still at the point where empirical research needs the guidance of a theory composed from refined observation. But, as I have observed—perhaps by now too frequently for readers' patience—we have lacked a theory of educational development that would provide such guidance.

At this point, then, it will probably not come as a surprise that I claim the stages outlined earlier do provide us with some guidance to the identification of certain important sensitive periods in educational development. In short, I am claiming that the four stages of educational development are in fact sensitive periods for the development of the capacities characteristic of each stage. That is, if, for example, the development of very general abstract schemes is characteristic of the philosophic stage, that stage is the sensitive period during which, for optimal educational development, that capacity must develop.

## Content

I have already argued that this theory shows the content/process distinctions often made in recent educational literature are empty. It makes no sense to try to give greater weight, or preference, to one over the other. Content is the fuel of the process; without content the capacities that ideally develop during the process of education cannot be actualized—as the child who does not inhabit a language-using environment cannot actualize linguistic capacities. Or, to continue with some of the terms used above, if a sensitive period represents the time during which the particular genes are responsive to relevant stimuli, optimal development requires that those stimuli be optimally accessible during the period. If the critical period is the philosophic stage, the relevant stimuli are general schemes. That is, content is the environment that stimulates or evokes the formative reaction of the organism's development of particular capacities.

An inquiry into the main sensitive periods of the process of educational development, then, should include consideration of what kinds of content are required for optimally encouraging the development of the appropriate capacities at the appropriate stages. That is, what things should we teach and in what order?

Given this theory as sketched so far, we would expect the characteristics of the stages to determine *how* content was to be organized rather than *what* content should be organized—especially in light of the claim that almost any content could be organized appropriately for any stage. But some principles may be derived from the characteristics of the stages that will go some way toward specifying appropriate content. In some cases, certain content will be more amenable to being organized for one stage rather than another. For example, dinosaurs make an immediate dramatic appeal to young children. There is nothing inherent in dinosaurs that makes them less relevant to any other stage, but their simple mythic appeal makes their appearance in the early grades sensible. In some cases, certain content may require the development of certain capacities before it becomes fully meaningful. For example, to speculate not entirely without reason, one might expect the sensitive period for learning the language of mathematics—as distinct from manipulating basic computations—to be during the romantic stage, accompanying and reflecting the increasing mastery of abstractions. If understanding of, say, calculus, requires the use of abstracting capacities, we may see it as content appropriate to the romantic stage.

The stages *determine how* content should be organized; fairly frequently they *influence what* content is most appropriate or *determine the kind* of content that is most appropriate; and, occasionally, as in the example of calculus, they *determine what* content is appropriate. The organization of content has been dealt with in the first four chapters, so here I will concentrate on the other two categories—the *what* rather than the *how*.

Below, I will take the stages one by one, discuss what capacities each is the sensitive period for the development of, and consider what kind of content best encourages that development.

## MYTHIC

### Sensitive period

Put most generally, this is the period of development during which it is important for the child to establish conceptual connections between the self and the world, for the child to be able to translate things in the world into conceptual entities and manipulate them flexibly. I described it earlier as the stage at which the child projects inner categories onto the outer world, thereby investing the world with meaning in those terms that are first and preeminently meaningful.

Prior to the mythic stage the infant has to master the range of early biological adaptations and the basic cognitive skills on which all future educational development depends. Inadequate development of the capacity for form recognition, for example, may largely determine later inability to read fluently. Greater or lesser success in making these early adaptations and mastering the basic cognitive skills will largely determine how responsive the child will be to the world. If one were to seek a general characterization for the pre-mythic stage, one might call it the sensitive period for finding the world interesting and establishing personal meaning within it. Lack of success here leads to more or less dullness, apathy, lack of interest in the world, and it undermines the possibility of any substantial educational development.

The critical development during the mythic stage is an extension of this earlier process of establishing personal meaning. I have characterized it as the stage during which the child learns, or fails to learn, how to use the world to think with. That is, the child learns first how to detach concepts from their exclusive inner associations, to attach them to things in the world, and gradually accommodate them to reflect more precisely the external things onto which they were projected. Increasingly through the mythic stage, then, the child develops the capacity to manipulate the outside world in the mind. The development of this capacity provides a fundamental intellectual confidence and security that the world *can* be made comprehensible. If this confidence is not achieved during the mythic stage, the person will always feel more or less intellectually insecure.

## Content

An important tool for, and product of, learning at each stage is some development in language. Flexible and sophisticated language use in general correlates highly with an ability to master typical content. This theory, however, suggests ways in which we might be more precise in specifying particular linguistic forms whose mastery would best contribute to learning the kind of content appropriate to particular stages. Or, to put it another way, it suggests desirable characteristics of the linguistic environment that will encourage the optimal unfolding of the appropriate capacities. I will, then, introduce discussion of appropriate content for each stage by commenting briefly on language. I am not arguing that mastery of these linguistic forms should precede mastery of particular kinds of content, rather, ideally, they will be acquired together. I separate them here only for purposes of description.

Given the characteristics of the mythic stage outline in chapter 1, what kind of linguistic developments should be encouraged to best help the child's mastery of them? First, a language rich in contrasts: good/bad, and the endless derivatives from these protagonists in the universal drama; contrasts of size, of importance, of speed, of all kinds of physical properties. The poles of the contrasts may be further enriched by encouraging their presentation in vivid and dramatic terms, moving the child from "very, very, very, very big" to "as big as a giant on top of the tallest tree on a mountain on daddy's head," or from "ever so, ever so green" to "as green as fresh grass on a summer morning in the shade of a leafy tree surrounded by green hills by a green lake." One may encourage children to elaborate any quality or property they mention in this way, making it a challenge to the imagination.

While encouraging elaboration, one should also encourage qualification, and thereby, precision. From big/small one should help students master as many distinct terms on the continuum of scale as possible. This might be begun during a class lesson by the teacher drawing a line across the chalkboard, marking "most big" at one end, and "most small" at the other. The class may be challenged to fill in as many additional points as possible, or be asked where they think "medium," "tiny," "huge," "enormous," "large," and so on, might fit. Similar continua could be constructed using elaborations and qualifications of fast/slow, strong/weak, and so on. The results might be transferred to long sheets of paper stuck on the wall. To these the children might add further terms as they hear them, and to which any new terms of scale might be referred when they arise. Such abstract continua will also lead easily to considerations of relativity, the actual meaning of the words in terms of real size depending on the things they are applied to—a huge mouse and a small elephant.[4]

Similarly the language of emotions and morality should begin from a clear sense of polar contrasts and should be increasingly elaborated and qualified. Also as the child moves through the mythic stage, the language of time should be developed. Under general divisions of past/future, with a line for present, the children can try to agree on the placing of "recently," "long ago," "soon,"

---

[4]These will hardly come as bright new ideas to any elementary-school teacher. I am mentioning them here not as new ideas but simply to draw attention to the kinds of linguistic developments that will support educational development through this stage.

"often" (frequent lines in a particular color). They may fill in various time-lines for their day, their year, their lives, their parents' lives, and so on.

As children approach the romantic stage, linguistic forms that will help them articulate their growing sense of the outside world's autonomy should be encouraged. Typically we make sense of things outside in terms of their effect on our senses; the continua of say hot/cold, hard/soft, big/small, fast/slow are based on us as the norm. Perception of the world as autonomous will be helped if we introduce language derived from less subjective scales. Thus objective measures of temperature, scale, speed, of landforms and climate should be introduced at the end of the mythic stage. Ideally, during the romantic stage, these kinds of perceptions will be mastered, as will more objective use of the language of physical properties.

While mentioning language more or less apart from content, it might be worth adding a word about the importance of those larger universal linguistic forms—stories. In earlier chapters I wrote a good deal about the story form, but very little about fictional stories. At this point, then, I would like to add a recommendation, not just that the story form be used pervasively at the mythic stage, but that fictional stories form a substantial part of the curriculum at the mythic stage. Ideally, these should move from fairly simple fairy stories for children at the beginning of the mythic stage, to a gradual increase in sophistication of plot and reality of incident as the children approach the romantic stage. Stories are the most effective tools for making their content meaningful. They are also effective ways of introducing the concepts of otherness, by building into their structure notions of causality, logical relationships, the movement of time. The potential of fictional stories for clarifying the concepts of almost any curriculum area should not be underestimated or ignored.

So, what about content? What kind of knowledge will be most effective in promoting children's educational development? By the mythic stage children have begun the great adventure of trying to make cognitive sense of the experience of being human in the world.

Their most basic implicit question is, "What's it all about?" Now, we know what it's all about. There is no need to be handwringing, limpwristed, or pettifogging about it, or, worse, to try to hide it from children by keeping them in a never-never land of provincial trivia. What it's all about is a life and death struggle against ignorance, fear, poverty, and hatred; it's a struggle for security, love, confidence, and knowledge. And at its heart, whether one is atheist or religious, it is infused with mystery—most basically the mystery of why there is existence rather than non-existence. Children can have access to all of this in one form or another; to the sense of mystery at the heart of things, to the knowledge of good and evil, to the fears and struggles and successes in building and sustaining a society and a culture, to the fallibility and strength of individuals. Again, educational development comes in the elaboration and refinement of the most fundamental perceptions; we do not build toward these fundamental perceptions by means of provincial trivia.[5]

When children first come to school, the main categories they have for thinking and learning are those formed in the titanic struggles of early physiological adaptation and in early learning of the customs and relationships within their families and among their friends. The content they are most familiar with typically—unless they have come from families that have systematically introduced them to fairy stories and other kinds of knowledge about the outside world—is about the customs, manners, and facts from their local

[5] This may seem to echo Jerome Bruner's aim, "to give a student as quickly as possible a sense of the fundamental ideas of a discipline." (*The Process of Education* [Cambridge, Mass.: Harvard University Press, 1960], p. 3.) And obviously they have much in common as recommendations for curriculum planning. It is perhaps worth noting, however, that the similarity is arrived at from quite different directions. Bruner lays emphasis both on the structure of the discipline and the child's developing capacities to understand increasingly sophisticated structures. I think it is not unfair to observe, though, that it is the former which most interests him in the book. He relies on Piaget's stages for the latter, and the consequence of this I think is to impoverish the kinds of subject matter he can relate to the specific intellectual stages of students' development. Indeed his most persuasive examples of fundamental ideas of a discipline comprehensible to young children are given in the chapter prior to, and so independent of, his discussion of Piaget's stages. The basic difference of approach in this work is to make the structuring of subject matter *determined* by the structure of students' developing understanding.

environment. The initial educational task is to destroy the tyranny of this local knowledge over children's imaginations by introducing them to knowledge about the world that is in its dramatic power and human significance analogous to their own earlier inner struggles. That is, it is important to show children that the outside world offers precise analogues for their titanic inner struggles and that the world can be understood clearly and profoundly in those terms, by use of those categories that the child has already developed. For example, the struggles for survival, security, and relative independence that the child has gone through are analogous to the struggles that civilization, cultures, nations, and the careers of individuals have gone through. We may refine and elaborate such notions as we develop educationally, but the most fundamental understanding, that which makes the concepts meaningful, is there to be used and developed in the earliest grades.

The greatest present danger to children's educational development seems to me to be the prevalence and growth of a curriculum which seems intent on suppressing, burying, atrophying children's vivid forms of thinking in local detail and trivia. What life in the world is all about is not primarily the secure surface of daily routines and local custom. Underneath this is a history of titanic struggle. We do no service to children by introducing them only to the secure surface and not letting them see that what they have gone through as individuals, their society and culture has gone through in its own way.

I have stated a number of times that it is the organization of knowledge that is usually more significant than the particular content. In the next chapter, I will consider what particular knowledge from various curriculum areas best supports educational development through each stage. Here I want to indicate the kind of content that seems most obviously influenced or determined by the requirements of the stage.

The first principle of organization for the mythic stage for each curriculum area is that we should begin organizing the content from the most profound and dramatic distinctions, or binary oppositions, inherent in the material. This principle determines to a considerable degree how a lesson or unit is constructed and presented. But what kind of content most readily lends itself to encouraging the fullest development of the capacities of the mythic stage?

A central feature of the mythic curriculum could be the kind of material recommended in example 1.1 in chapter 1—the great true story of mankind in bold and dramatic outline. The content could be selected from the whole of history, and exemplify and elaborate binary opposites such as liberty/tyranny, knowledge/ignorance, creativity/conservatism, courage/cowardliness, heroes and heroines/ villains and fools, and so on.

An equivalent focus would be to characterize and elaborate the major contrasts in nature on the basis of hospitable/hostile, helpful/destructive, tame/wild, alive/inanimate, and so on. Such oppositions may be used to organize knowledge about the variety of dramatic differences in the natural world: the different forms of earth, air, fire, and water; the most dramatic interactions and relationships; the whirling planets and galaxies; the endless adaptability of living forms; the interacting cycles of living things, gases, and minerals; and so on. That is, the most basic natural forms and processes should be presented to children as the wonder they are and in a manner which encourages and makes habitual the persisting question, "Why are things the way they are?"

That kind of content may form the basis of a mythic curriculum. Without any very serious attempt to be comprehensive or systematic, children should be introduced and given clear access to the most dramatic and vivid things in history and nature. The first distinctions to establish, and elaborate from, in most curriculum areas are the most profound and basic ones.

In the attempt to stress what I consider most important, I have perhaps overused terms like *dramatic* and *dynamic* and *vivid*, until I have suggested an image of a classroom powerhouse from which children stagger shell-shocked every few hours, neurons popping with dramatic overload. Well, better that than its opposite, though the principles for which I have been arguing do not necessitate constant pyrotechnic activity from the teacher. The sense of drama is created by exposing the mythic qualities inherent in the material.


# ROMANTIC

## Sensitive period

At risk of tautology, the romantic stage is the sensitive period for the development of a sense of romance. And what is that, in educational terms? In chapter 2, I described the central characteristic of this stage as an ambivalent desire both to discover the limits of reality and the possible and, yet, to transcend them; a desire to transcend the world while yet remaining in it—to be both Clark Kent and Superman.

It is no coincidence that the kind of comic characters of most interest at the mythic stage are humanized animals, unreal creatures, who mediate between those polar opposites nature/culture. At the romantic stage interest turns to comic (or book, television, film) characters who have an everyday existence but also a transcendent one. The more grown-up the anticipated romantic audience, the more subtle the fusion of everyday and transcendent in the hero or heroine. During the mid-seventies in North America the two most obvious and popular romantic television characters for our techno-logical age were the six million dollar man and the bionic woman. As with Superman's birth and escape from the dying planet Krypton, so the etiology of the six million dollar man and the bionic woman are important for suggesting that they inhabit a real or possible world. It is this that defines them, in my terms, as romantic not mythic. No attempt is made to suggest a plausible or possible world in which Korky the Cat or Biffo the Bear live, dressed in normal clothes, standing on two legs, in a fairly normal middle-class environment.

The search for transcendence within reality is at the heart of romance. In educational terms, the search for the transcendent is the motivator for learning about great ideas, people, movements, natu-ral phenomena, and so on. It stimulates what I have called romantic associations with these. An important means of making these romantic associations is by imaginatively inhabiting these characters, ideas, movements and alien forms of life. So, in saying that this stage is the critical period for the development of a sense of romance, I am saying also that it is the critical period for developing the ability to make romantic associations with things in the real world that are outside everyday experience. And this, in turn, may be called the development of controlled imagination.[6]

## Content

The linguistic forms appropriate for best helping educational development through the romantic stage are largely implicit in the kind of content to be taught. That is, if they are learning about marine biology, they will learn the language appropriate to naming the life forms, their environment, processes of interaction, and so on. I will not then separate language from content for separate comment here, except to note that through the stage there should be developed increasingly abstract and general terms. Hand in hand with mastery of content will come elaboration and refinement of the terms that will allow increasingly precise descriptions of otherness—historical periods and different styles of life, geographical place and space, logical relationships—and increasingly refined articulation of emotion and belief.

We were led to a general area of appropriate content at the mythic stage by trying to help the child answer the implicit question, "What's it all about?" Similarly for the romantic stage, we might be able to identify a general area of appropriate content by finding the most general question implicit in its characteristics. We may state such a question as something like, "What are the limits and dimensions of the real and the possible?" The most appropriate

[6] I use the word controlled to distinguish it from the wilder, or freer, or more *sauvage* imagination of the mythic stage. That wilder imagination creates entities by mixing especially such categories as human/animal, human/vegetable, human/mineral—creating impossible beings like invisible people, talking trees or lamp posts, etc. At the romantic stage this free imagination becomes controlled and forged into a tool for exploring reality, for vivifying the inanimate and abstract and making them humanly meaningful.

content for the romantic stage will be that which will help students best answer this question. And what will that be?

We noted earlier that students' primary access to knowledge at this stage was through romantic associations with transcendent qualities. One might organize content at this stage using those transcendent qualities as themes. We might choose such themes as courage, genius, energy, creativity, adventure, and so on. These could be exemplified in each subject area. Different aspects of courage might be brought out in music, science, and history, but content could be chosen and organized to illustrate this quality in a way that would allow students to associate with it eagerly.

If access to knowledge comes primarily through transcendent human qualities, then, knowledge should be presented primarily as a product of the expression of those qualities. For example, in science teaching, the content should not be, as it usually is, dissociated from its human source and presented simply as a body of facts, processes, and methods of inquiry. Rather the content should be presented as the product of people's energy, persistence, genius, inquisitiveness and so on. Science is primarily a process whereby people secure knowledge, not an inert body of secured knowledge. It is a human activity, in which human hopes, fears, courage, energy are crucially involved.

One way to present scientific knowledge through the people and activities whereby it was secured, and so bring it to romantic life, is to follow the example of Professor Richard M. Eakin. The *Times Literary Supplement* suggested he receive a "constructive daftness prize of the year" for the way he taught the introductory zoology course at Berkeley.[7] I will simply quote a part of the 1976 *TLS* commentary:

> One day, without warning, the lucky students of Zoology 10 found themselves faced with a figure in full Tudor fig and wig. "Gracious Ladies and worthy Gentlemen," he began, "before presenting a discourse on the heart and the circulation of the

[7] Described in Richard M. Eakin, *Great Scientists Speak Again* (Berkeley: University of California Press, 1976).

blood, listen I pray you to some personal history. I was born on All Fools' Day 1578. . . ." Pulses quickened, absenteeism evaporated, and—though Professor Eakin is too modest to say so—grades doubtless soared. Heartened by his success, he has since added to his repertoire Darwin, Pasteur, Mendel, the experimental embryologist Spemann, and the U.S. army surgeon William Beaumont, whose classic studies of digestive physiology were greatly facilitated by observations on a wounded French-Canadian trapper with an obliging permanent opening to the stomach. This book, lavishly illustrated by entertaining photographs, brings Professor Eakin's mimeses to a larger audience. He admits to a relish for thick slices of centre-cut ham: Pasteur says "parbleu" from time to time, Mendel is a cigar-smoking Friar Tuck.

It is not difficult to become a guest-speaker in your own classroom. An old cloak, a peculiar hat, a bit of lace, a false beard, the most trivial attempt to suggest an illusion is enough. The students' imagination will fill in the rest. We are not all great actors, of course, but we do not need to be to achieve the desired effect. To make the slightest pretence, the occasional anachronism, the slightly foreign accent, will do the job. Nor need such a method be restricted to science. Beethoven, with discarded hearing aid, might introduce a symphony; Napoleon explain his hopes before Waterloo; Thomas Jefferson talk about relations with England; and so on. All the knowledge in the world is human knowledge, and each piece of it is part of the great adventure of the human mind. It is important that students get some sense of this.

The content influenced by the requirements of the romantic stage will be found by looking to the major expressions of human energy and creativity. The great things done and thought will best feed development through this stage: the building of the cathedrals and pyramids; the great scientific discoveries; the greatest works of music, literature, painting; the careers of great people. It will not greatly matter if the curriculum is not carefully organized at this stage to encourage synthesis. That will happen best during the next stage. What matters here is to give students access to the widest possible range of knowledge and encourage them to develop a sense of the romance of man's intellectual, as well as all the other, adventures. By this means, the romantic stage involves a dialectical extension of the student's concepts, feelings, and other human qualities by constant comparisons with, and inhabitation of, other people's in other times and places.

One often hears from teachers that it is impossible to provide typical high school students with access to appreciation of the work of, say, Giotto, or even Michelangelo. Yet according to my above claims, these should form the core of a romantic curriculum. It is surely true that attempting to introduce children to such art works by showing them and pointing out their glories will leave our image-saturated students cold. But if one introduces them by means of the lives of Giotto or Michelangelo—in the context of what preceded them, the size of the challenge they faced, the daring and courage they showed, the degree of their originality, the opposition and difficulties they overcame—then one may provide the human context that makes humanly meaningful the otherwise inhuman marks of paint or shaped stone.

## PHILOSOPHIC

### Sensitive period

During the philosophic stage, students search for general truths about the way the world works, the way people are, the way things happen. It is a period during which students' minds struggle to bring all the things they know together, focused on themselves. It is the sensitive period for the development of the capacity to seek and find general patterns, regularities, laws in complex phenomena; the capacity to organize complex phenomena into causal processes; the capacity to bind all their knowledge and experience into a single whole; the capacity to find unity underlying diversity; the capacity to form ideologies and metaphysical visions. It is, in short, the sensitive period for developing the capacity to generate, what I call in chapter 3, general schemes.

Uncontrolled by the capacities of the ironic stage, the generalizing activities of the philosophic stage tend to get out of hand, reducing everything to simplistic schemes. It is this tendency that makes teaching at this stage so irritating to so many mature scholars. In an attempt to curb this tendency they try to introduce the ironic capacities that control such generalizing. This control, if introduced too early, will be achieved at the expense of the capacities it is supposed to control. First the generalizing capacities must be developed and exercised. Thereafter, and only thereafter, control may be learned. The philosophic stage is the critical period for the development and exercise of this generalizing capacity. Any inquiry that is to be serious and not get lost under uncontrollable detail, unable to see wood for trees, requires the development of the capacities of the philosophic stage.

## Content

Given the characteristics of the philosophic stage outlined in chapter 3, what linguistic forms will best help their development? It will be a language rich in abstractions, in the terms of metaphysics, ideology, general theories of artistic, literary, and scientific progress. It will find a prominent place for the names of the categories used in the theories of people like Northrop Frye,[8] Eric Auerbach,[9] Thomas Kuhn,[10] Ernst Gombrich,[11] Bruno Snell.[12] It will be attracted by the most powerful organizing concepts of sociology, anthropology, psychology, and what I am tempted to call metaphilosophy. A language that is rich in terms and that will allow as many distinctions as possible at this level of refined abstraction will help students make their general schemes more sophisticated.

As with the previous stages, it might help to try to identify the

---

[8] Northrop Frye, *The Anatomy of Criticism* (Princeton: Princeton University Press, 1957).

[9] Erich Auerbach, *Mimesis*, trans. Willard R. Trask (Princeton: Princeton University Press, 1955).

[10] Thomas S. Kuhn, *The Structure of Scientific Revolutions*, International Encyclopedia of Unified Science, vol. 2, no. 2 (Chicago: University of Chicago Press, 1962).

[11] E. H. Gombrich, *Art and Illusion* (Princeton: Princeton University Press, 1960).

[12] Bruno Snell, *The Discovery of the Mind*, trans. T. G. Rosenmeyer (Oxford: Blackwell Publisher, 1953).

kind of question implicit in students' interest in knowledge at this stage. Such a question as, "What is the truth about the causal processes whereby the world works?" seems to represent their focus of inquiry fairly well.

As argued in chapter 3, we come to precision and respect for particularity not directly, but through the general. One thing that seems clear from attempts to simulate intelligent behavior by machines is that humans seem to compose meaning in a manner fundamentally different from the early attempts to produce examples of artificial intelligence. Machines and computers compose meaningful patterns from bits; that is, they add the bits up into something, such that the whole is precisely the sum of the parts (to use somewhat tendentious language). The human mind seems to work quite differently, it composes meaning by identifying the bits within a pattern or context. That is, somehow we see a general pattern or context within which and by means of which and from which the elements that make it up derive meaning. Particular meaning and context or general pattern are woven intricately together. It is this that has made it so difficult to get machines to perform what are casual functions to humans—mastery of grammar, translation, etc.

On the larger scale of educational development, the same principle seems to hold true. We begin mastery of detailed truths about the world with a general orientation within the limits or parameters of the real (romantic stage), followed by an attempt to characterize the general processes and major aspects or features of the real during the philosophic stage, and only then do we make an attempt to perceive and value particular truths for their own sake. Given that we find particulars meaningful only by locating them within a context, we must first establish as clear an image of the contexts as possible.

The content that is of most importance for the philosophic stage then is that which best enables students to compose or to see general organizing schemes in each field of inquiry. Subjects should be introduced through the most powerful organizing theories, from an examination of their most determining presuppositions and assumptions. I am perhaps overly sensitive to the likelihood that this recommendation will run against the grain of many scholars. This kind of generalizing is considered dangerous, indeed it can be quite intoxicating, leading students to wild generalization and crazy theorizing. My observation is that this kind of activity is good and educationally appropriate; the only defence against its excesses is a large and constantly enlarging data-base. Generalizing on a slender data-base leads to becoming "horribly mad", and, unless the data-base can be expanded, staying "horribly mad". But there is no educationally sane defence in trying to steer students away from or around, or to suppress this impulse to generalization. The only way ahead is through it.

If we steer students into the most appropriate content for developing the capacities of this stage, we will be steering them in social studies, for example, toward the kind of metahistorical inquiries outlined in example 3.2. In physics and geography, we will guide them toward cosmological and cosmogonic speculation, and provide access to as much data as we can that will inform and support such speculation. General theories about fundamental particles and astrophysics—quarks and black holes together—will provide aliments to philosophic development and will stimulate further inquiry into the details of those topics. Fashion and why it changes; architectural and artistic styles and their development; myths and the human mind; truth in fiction and history; the existence or otherwise of God; meaning in music; psychoanalysis versus behaviorism as therapies; why civilizations developed in the middle east; and similar very general philosophic inquiries should fill the curriculum at this stage. The move to particularity will come as a result of the intoxication offered by such general inquiries.

Students at this stage will be attracted to what used to be known, and still is known outside universities, as philosophy; the kind of philosophy that attempts to address directly questions like, "What is the meaning of life?" "What is truth, beauty, humor?" "What is justice and how should one organize a just society?" "How far should the individual good be sacrificed to the good of all?"

It is perhaps worth stating that I think the mature competent

philosopher needs to have passed through this stage no less than anyone else. To rush the student of philosophy away from such questions and toward the most rigorous analytic philosophy leads to the
production of pedants who cannot see any more general use for
philosophy than the application of their analytic skills to a limited
set of fashionable topics. Productive and rigorous philosophy will
come rather from the refinement of those same skills as a result of
intoxication with general questions and the sobering dissatisfaction
that results from dealing with them in a philosophic manner. In the
process of becoming dissatisfied, however, is the development of the
capacity to seek the typical, the recurrent, and to scan constantly and
flexibly for ways to create more general meaning. This capacity will
then be controlled by ironic rigor, but it will have been developed.

    We will want to direct students toward what are commonly
called interdisciplinary topics. As I have outlined content for the
previous stages they may seem to be all more or less interdisciplinary. I would rather call them *predisciplinary*. Disciplined study
is *achieved*. The disciplinary distinctions common in our most
advanced institutions of learning become only gradually appropriate distinctions in ways of learning and knowing. During the mythic
stage, disciplinary distinctions, except in the very broadest terms, are
largely irrelevant. During the romantic stage they become, at most
refined, convenient ways of organizing knowledge. The philosophic
is the stage during which the reasons for disciplinary distinctions
begin to become articulate and meaningful. As with development in
general, they become articulated *out of* a more or less indistinct
general field; as the field is brought into more precise focus, as it
were, the lines and divisions become more distinct. Disciplinary
distinctions become meaningful, however, within the general field—
if one has no sense of the general field, the divisions will be largely
meaningless; superstitious touchstones of security, rather than
clearly understood boundaries. Scholars who have been rushed
through the romantic and philosophic stages are often the most
religiously dedicated to preservation of their discipline boundaries,
because in the most profound sense they do not know their meaning

and purpose. They know only that beyond these secure boundaries there be dragons and monsters.

I would prefer to call the kinds of general inquiries I have recommended for the philosophic stage, *predisciplinary*. *Inter*disciplinary understanding comes only after mastery of more than one discipline, and it is the term I would rather see reserved for those major and important contributions to understanding made by the most accomplished scholars. In these terms, interdisciplinary understanding is not normally achieved at the philosophic stage, but predisciplinary inquiries that do not pay full respect to the disciplinary distinctions and their refined methodologies are appropriate. Indeed, they are the necessary means of developing that respect and mastering those refined methodologies.

The remaining point to repeat about content at the philosophic stage is that for best educational development there needs to be a lot of it. For students to be able to form powerful general schemes, they require a lot of knowledge. Impoverished general schemes—the clichés of bar and television talkshows—follow from little knowledge, for which they may be true and adequate. Rich and powerful general schemes, that have the energy to drive students through this stage to mature irony, can *only* be built on rich and varied knowledge.

# IRONIC

## Sensitive period

The ironic stage is the sensitive period for the development of two associated capacities: first, the capacity to accept the primacy of particular truths in the composition of meaning, and, second, the capacity to control the capacities of all the previous stages. Together these provide an important intellectual freedom; a freedom from the self and its immature needs.

In each of the previous stages, particular truths about the world were always to some degree subservient in the composition of meaning to some mental form; that is, the world was made to conform with either the mythic need to collapse things to a relatively small set of internally derived categories, or the romantic need to select only those things that fed a sense of transcendence, or the philosophic need to fit things to a general scheme. At the ironic stage, mental forms are made to conform to the particular truths established about the world and experience. That is, only at the ironic stage can people realistically hope to provide an objective mental image of the world, unfettered by the distortions caused by the uncontrolled characteristics of the previous stages.

Clearly the ironic control of the capacities of the previous stages will never be absolute, and to the degree that ironic capacities are less than one-hundred percent developed, the narcissistic distortions of the previous stages will interfere with the ironic respect for the world's objective existence and the ultimate ironic capacity to see things as they are.

The struggle at the ironic stage is to bend, twist, elaborate, and proliferate, mental forms to more precisely body forth particular truths about the world and experience. Self-conscious control of all the capacities of the previous stages then[13] allows the composition of larger meaning by careful induction from the secured particulars. By using philosophic capacities under ironic control, for example, the person may construct a very general theory, rivalling in power the most general philosophic schemes. The difference will be that the general theory at the ironic stage will follow from, be sensitive to, be flexible and responsive to particulars. At the philosophic stage, the student's commitment keeps the general scheme rigid; at the ironic stage, the commitment is to the particulars.

## Content

The capacities of the ironic stage imply no particular kinds of content. Anything goes. The only principles seem to be that the

---

[13] I do not mean "then" in a temporal sense. Again for purposes of description I am separating complex processes that seem more or less simultaneous and woven together.

ironic person works for an increasing mastery of something in particular, to forge new intellectual tools for better representing some particular truth about the world or experience. That is, there will be an intense, but not exclusive, specialization.

Being not exclusive simply means that along with an area of steadily increasing mastery, the ironic person will have a lively interest in just about everything, and will maintain an ongoing familiarity with just about everything to the degree that this is possible.

## CONCLUSION

My claim here is that the stages I have characterized are sensitive periods in human educational development, similar in kind to the critical periods identified by genetic biologists. Clearly this claim is insecure, my concern here is simply to establish its plausibility in a form that will open it to empirical test. If it is true it is extremely important. The degree of its plausibility suggests it is worth testing.

What will make such tests quite difficult to conduct validly is the fact that the further from birth humans get, the more diffuse seem to be the sensitive periods. In the earliest biological adaptions, the sensitive periods seem quite precise in the time of their opening and closing; we are responsive to the relevant stimuli, whether forms or sentences, between relatively clearly defined periods after birth. But the stages I have been characterizing seem to open at different times for different people, take different amounts of time from opening to closing, the appropriate capacities are developed in different degrees and at different speeds and in different ways, and the process may be minimally begun by some people and largely completed by others.

These are severe problems. It is only if they are so overwhelming that this theory cannot be verified or falsified at all, however, that potential difficulties with empirical validation make a theory worthless. I think this theory, while presenting problems to the researcher and calling for imaginative invention, is far from this situation.

One part of the plausibility of the claims in this chapter turns on the similarity between the processes whereby critical periods are seen in biological adaptations and changes in our focus of interest, our interest in kinds of knowledge, and our use of knowledge may be seen in later educational development. To quote, rather than paraphrase, as earlier, W. Ragan Callaway, Jr.:

> A critical period inheres in the fact that the applicable genes are usually responsive to relevant stimuli for a limited period of time. It follows that the same stimulation before or after the [critical] period invariably will have *less* and possibly will have no effect in realizing such competencies.[14]

The four sensitive periods of educational development, unlike the more precise sensitive or critical periods of the early years, may be responsive to particular kinds of knowledge environments that will stimulate and evoke them for long periods of time. The particular time when, say, the romantic critical period is stimulated may depend a lot on how adequately the mythic critical period has developed. We seem to retain the potential to move into, say, the philosophic stage over a period of years. It may be held latent, without danger, until the appropriate environmental stimuli activate it. There do, however, seem to be limits, even though the older we become the more broad they become. At this point, it seems difficult to be very precise about those limits. At the beginning of each of the first four chapters, I have indicated what seems to me the range of normal ages for the opening and closing of each stage, given an appropriately stimulating environment. I find it difficult to guess what might be the age *limits* for each stage. I suspect that by the age of twenty, say, the critical periods for developing mythic and romantic capacities have usually closed. By that age, people might engage mythic and romantic content as entertaining, but it will no longer be serving as aliments to further development.

The process of developing through preprogrammed sensitive

---

[14] W. Ragan Callaway, Jr., *Modes of Biological Adaptation and Their Role in Intellectual Development,* Perceptual Cognitive Development Monographs, vol. 1, no. 1 (The Galton Institute, 1970).

periods by means of particular kinds of knowledge environments adds a dimension to the notion of educational development being a process of dialectical interaction between knowledge and mind. The developmental process will not work itself out independently of an appropriately organized knowledge environment, and inappropriately organized knowledge will be ineffective at stimulating development.

# 7

# CURRICULUM AREAS

So far, in characterizing the four stages of educational development, I have used examples drawn from the history curriculum. My claim, however, is that the stages are valid for describing the general process of education. That is, though the stages are descriptive of a process resulting from a dialectical interaction between intellectual development and the growing mastery of curriculum content, the process so far outlined is not only valid in terms of developing understanding of history. In this chapter, the stages will be detached from history and will be applied to other curriculum areas. I will consider this developmental theory in relation to the English/language arts and the science curricula. I will look at these through the stages as outlined above and see whether the result is not a more sensible way of organizing English/language arts and science curricula in order to lead people to a more flexible and sophisticated understanding of both areas.

## ENGLISH/LANGUAGE ARTS
### Introduction

In general, people tend toward abbreviation of language. It is easier to say that we intend to teach someone to read or to write than to say that we intend to teach them to read or to write something. What is the difference? A subtle but potentially important matter of focus or emphasis. If one thinks in terms of teaching someone to read or to write, one's focus will likely be on teaching the technical aspects of reading and writing, on the mastery of techniques and skills. If one thinks always of teaching to read something or to write something, one shifts the focus onto just what it is the particular learners should be reading or writing in the process of acquiring the skills. That is, we draw attention constantly to the purpose for mastery of techniques and to the immediate practical value of them.

Thinking in terms of teaching children decoding and encoding skills, may make us feel in possession of a more scientific approach, but it tends to focus attention even more narrowly on contentless technique. If we think in terms of teaching reading and writing about significant ideas and experiences, we focus on what kinds of ideas and experiences can be put into words to make the acts of reading and writing worthwhile. It is useful to remember that most people most of the time have not been literate and that literacy is a limited value in human experience. It is not absolutely important that children learn to read or to write or decode and encode. These skills have particular uses and values, and our sense of these limited values should serve to guide children and adults to the something they will find most educationally beneficial.

My stages are less directly relevant to teaching decoding and encoding skills than to identifying the range of something that will make the hierarchy of literacy skills seem worth mastering. I am claiming that the particular method used in teaching is a lot less significant than the ideas or experiences contained in the words chosen in the process of using whatever method. Given the prerequisite intellectual development, learning to read or to write is easy. Though they may be remarkably complex tasks, humans bring to these tasks even more remarkably complex mental equipment which makes the tasks, literally, child's play. The complexity of the tasks should not deceive us into thinking they are difficult to master. Given that an average child has superabundant intellectual capacity to learn to read and to write well, the primary task is simply to make these activities seem worthwhile to the child.

With regard to English, then, these stages will guide us toward things that will make reading and writing seem worthwhile. If we can provide children, students, and adults at each stage with what is most engaging and educationally beneficial, skills will develop largely incidentally.

## Mythic

English/language arts is important to the child's educational development because it is the curriculum subject most centrally concerned with the development of those imaginative projections which are fundamental to adequate development of the capacities of the mythic stage.[1]

Fairy tales, fables—any stories with the mythic characteristics outlined in chapter 1—are educationally vital. Stories are often viewed as incidentals or as rewards for good work at dull technical exercises. I would put stories at the heart of elementary English. If children's minds are caught up by the worlds of imaginative projection—that first dynamic release from the smothering and unhandleable self—and they learn that reading can provide them with access to these worlds at any time, they will learn to read.

It is not, I think, merely coincidental that children master and are engaged by the story form as they master, and take pleasure in

---

[1] While one may sensibly doubt the easy application of Freudian dogma, Bruno Bettleheim makes a case for the *psychological* importance of fairy tales that overlaps to a fair degree with what I am claiming is their *educational* importance. These are obviously not mutually exclusive categories. See *The Uses of Enchantment* (New York: Knopf, 1976).

using, the sentence form. A number of students of poetics see the story as simply the sentence writ large.[2] Stories and sentences seem to be an expression at different levels of narrative units of the same mental characteristics. Mastery of the rhythms of the story will probably contribute to greater sophistication and mastery of the sentence form. It is not coincidental that mastery of the story and the sentence form occur together. Nursery rhymes, for example, are incomplete fragmented stories and appeal most strongly during the period when the child's mastery of the sentence is also incomplete and speech comes in fragmented sentences. This common development seems to be maintained throughout our lives; from simple complete stories and simple complete sentences we move to understanding sophisticated stories and sophisticated sentences, and on to the amazingly sophisiticated parodies on story and sentence in a book like *Finnegans Wake*.

Stories should not be considered casual entertainment. They are embodiments of fundamental structures of the human mind; they reflect and educate us in important ways of making sense of experience, of investing the world with meaning, and of putting world and experience into words.

Achieving a satisfactory, and satisfying, story form requires discipline; it requires a conscious structuring of a set of bits—events, characters, descriptions—into a coherent whole. It is useful to consider the bits and the whole separately for a moment in order to show that what may seem to be conflicting principles are in fact consistent. When children are encouraged to write, tell, act out stories of their own invention, one should encourage wild metaphoric associations, untrammeled imagination, and as much freedom as possible in the articulation of the bits. In moulding these bits into a coherent story one should encourage discipline and the imposition of formal constraints. That is, one does not curtail

---

[2] See for example Roland Barthes, "Introduction a l'analyse structurale des récits," *Communications* 8 (1966); A. J. Greimas, "Eléments pour une théorie de l'interpretation du récits mythique," *Communications* 8 (1966); and Tzvetan Todorov, *Grammaire du Décaméron* (The Hague: Mouton, 1969).

imaginative play with the bits by showing that a larger kind of meaning may be achieved by composing them into an effective story, and one does not allow undisciplined expression by letting the child be satisfied with only imaginative play. Thus, one teaches that one kind of meaning and pleasure belongs to particular imaginative play, and this contributes toward the larger meaning and pleasure that only the complete story can achieve.

It should be noted, too, that following a story involves other skills the English/language arts curriculum aims at. Being able to follow a story requires a sense of logical sequences of causality, problem solving, analyzing events and situations, forming hypotheses and reformulating them in light of further knowledge, and so on. Learning the conventions of increasingly sophisticated story forms *is* learning such intellectual skills.

What this theory suggests for the day to day practical work of developing literacy skills is first this emphasis on the *kind* of stories referred to in chapter 1. English should be thought of as the time for hearing, writing, inventing, acting out, stories.

What follows for more detailed technical work at skills promotion is the suggestion that such exercises should as far as possible be put into the context of such stories. For example, workbooks that have lists of more or less discrete exercises will tend to be less effective than workbooks that contain all the same exercises but welded into story forms, with elements of puzzle solving. Such stories could be very brief—jokes or fables can be ideal. I will discuss the puzzle-solving or game-playing aspect more extensively below in the section on sciences. But it is worth noting here that games that have a binary drama, with the expectation of victory or defeat, or the possibility of achieving or failing to achieve some goal, with an end that satisfies, can also be powerful educational tools for literacy skill development. Skill acquisition that depends on episodic exercises, which are justified to the child on the grounds that a future literacy will open up great riches, will tend to be relatively ineffective. It is potentially true, of course, but meaningless to the child unless the immediate practical activity is also perceived as worthwhile and engaging.

## Romantic

Much of the above is relevant also to the romantic stage, though the kinds of stories appropriate here are the more sophisticated kind that have the characteristics outlined in chapter 2. This is a period for the increasing sophistication of writing skills. These skills are developed best by practice, by writing a lot. As long as students are writing and reading what best engages them at this stage, such writing will not appear just a chore. The themes for essays and stories should be romantic themes, with sloshing sentimentality. Stories and essays should relate to those themes indicated in chapter 2 as most appropriate for engaging, and developing the capacities of, students at the romantic stage.

The writing of poetry should also be encouraged, with the clear agreement that the product need not be made public if the student does not wish it. The reading of poetry and learning it by heart is also important during this stage; it will extend the range of students' rhythms of language, sentiment and emotion. They should not be encouraged to appreciate the best poetry. The best poetry for children at the romantic stage is romantic poetry. More sophisticated poetry will become accessible only after they have gone through the appreciation of romantic poetry. It will remain inaccessible as poetry during the romantic stage however much time and ingenuity is spent by the teacher in explicating it.

From the simplest romantic poetry—one thinks of, for boys, Thomas Macauley's *Lays of Ancient Rome* or other poems that have strong rhythms[3] and a strong narrative line developing some romantic theme—one should move to those poems that contain aliments to more sophisticated appreciation. Poets like Rudyard Kipling or G. K. Chesterton or A. E. Housman, for example, write fairly straightforward romantic poems, which nevertheless contain elements of more sophisticated philosophic themes.

The assumption that children or students whose appreciation

[3] Rhythm is a kind of contentless story. By convention it sets up expectations, which are complicated and resolved.

of poetry is immature require simpler poems often leads to the selection of poems that appear to have relatively simple themes. Often, however, such poems—about things like how beautiful daffodils and nature are—have very little *romantic* appeal. That is, it's not the *simplicity* of the theme that counts, but its *romanticism*. For example, the idea of nature in its quotidian forms being beautiful is an ironic appreciation, largely inaccessible to students at the romantic stage. It is rather the remote and the rare, the mountains of the moon, the valley of the shadows, that will appeal to the romantic imagination in a way that Derwent waters cannot. The main characteristics of romantic poetry are strong rhythms, a story line, heroic characters doing something heroic, human qualities *in extremis*, some degree of sentimentality, high drama or humour.

As during the mythic stage, a romantic wildness, freedom and expansion needs to be encouraged, along with increasing discipline over form and manner of writing or reading. Quite commonly proponents of freedom for students' expression fail to recognize that disciplined mastery of a medium is a prerequisite for freedom of expression. Such people observe that disciplined mastery of, say, the details of grammar are not important for the ability to best express oneself; James Joyce, for example, ignored all such rules. It needs to be stressed, however, that Joyce did not write the way he did out of ignorance of rules and usage, but because his mastery of conventions was so complete that he could transcend them. One cannot transcend conventional forms until one has thoroughly mastered them.

## Philosophic

Though the writing of essays will ideally have been common during the romantic stage, those essays will have been relatively simple, and their form will have been significantly determined by their theme, which will have ensured the essays still remain quite close to being stories. Though the essay form and story form have much in common at the level of structure, in their sophisticated stages, they deal with different kinds of units. At an early romantic stage, essays will properly be largely concerned with people, events, emotion—the stuff of stories. In the more sophisticated philosophic stage, they will be concerned largely with arguments and ideas. The philosophic stage may be considered as primarily the period during which students master the techniques of rhetoric.

During this stage, poetry and fiction will tend to play a *relatively* less prominent role in students' imaginative lives, and ideas will play a *relatively* more prominent role. A stress on rhetoric represents an acknowledgment of this and trains the student in further nuances of language, forms of argument, presentation of arguments, and the techniques of persuasion. It is in these that the students are interested and by these that their literary and linguistic education may proceed.

Essay writing assignments should be put into the context of persuading someone of something the student cares about. Essay writing should no longer be considered an activity that is restricted to the school, but should be aimed outward. An essay might be addressed to a corporation, a store, a government agency, a newspaper, a politician, a television station, a newspaper organized by the students, and so on. The students' arguments have to be felt to be having an effect on the world or they will not satisfy the students' developing sense of themselves as social and political agents. If the art of fiction requires organizing events into a powerful story, so the art of rhetoric involves composing arguments into a powerful essay.

During this period, students should engage frequently in formal debates. Informal classroom discussions will be less educationally important at this stage than the carefully prepared formal debate, which will also elicit and exercise the techniques of rhetoric.

The literature that appeals to this stage has been discussed briefly in chapter 3. It is, primarily, a literature of ideas. A writer like Jorge Luis Borges ideally reflects a pure philosophic expression. Typically, of course, students will not be pure in this sense; they will retain the capacities developed during the romantic and mythic stages, and literature with romantic and mythic qualities will potentially appeal to them. The more they are involved in developing the capacities of the philosophic stage, however, the more they will tend to reject mythic and romantic literature as not serious and unsophisticated—appropriate perhaps as bedtime reading but not engaging their best capacities.

The teacher's role in developing the student's powers of rhetoric is as a refiner, a suggester of new strategies and techniques, or counter-arguer and critic.

### Ironic

At this stage people need only guidance from someone more experienced; guidance, that is, as to what kinds of books they might enjoy. Literary skills should become increasingly refined by practice and should be flexible enough to be suitable for a wide range of different tasks, from writing letters to persuading politicians, to selling furniture, to writing novels, and so on.

## FOREIGN LANGUAGES

It is worth noting that the same introductory point made above about English/language arts applies equally well to foreign languages. If we think in terms of teaching someone French or Spanish, we focus again on the technical aspects of the task. If we try to think always of teaching someone to say *something* or to read *something* in French or Spanish, we focus on the thing that will motivate people to want to learn the language and that will engage them in trying to abstract meaning from the language.

## SCIENCE

### Introduction

The image of science most commonly presented to children and students is of a secure and objective body of knowledge, the discovery of pieces of which is represented as a linear sequence stretching back from the present and which is projected into the future in terms of technological innovations. This falsifies the nature of science and the reality of scientific progress, and abstracts from science the excitement and human qualities which can make it most readily accessible to children.

The falsification of scientific progress comes from presenting it in terms of the discovery of bits of knowledge that gradually accumulate to the present scientific methodology and worldview.[4] The byways and dead ends are ignored, as though the single broad highway of scientific progress which we impose when looking back from the present was the only possible alternative. Much of the modern opposition and fear of science seems to follow from this school-encouraged image of a relentless and inhuman juggernaut. Much of students' fascination with magic and superstition and their susceptibility to magic and mystical knowledge charlatanry seems largely due to their having gained no clear sense of what science is and of how it is a much wilder and more exciting adventure for the human mind than the tired nonsense offered so liberally on every paperback stand.

The main contribution of this stage theory to science teaching is its ability to suggest *how* science may be represented to children and students as the most exciting adventure humans have ever launched. In general, movement through the stages should be paralleled by approaches to science appropriate to the intellectual characteristics of each stage. This movement will follow the general scheme developed in the first four chapters. It will be no use to try to impress on young children or students a rigorous and proper scientific approach—which is essentially an achievement of the ironic intelligence. Modern scientific understanding is an achievement only gradually attained by the human race, it cannot be grasped whole by young children. They must go through stages of increasingly greater understanding of science that will in a simplified way recapitulate one feature of the process whereby the race has attained its present more mature scientific understanding.

As with social studies, people tend to confuse the dimension in

[4]Whatever else may be doubtful in Thomas S. Kuhn, *The Structure of Scientific Revolutions* (Chicago: University of Chicago Press, 1962), he shows clearly how the history of science tends to be falsified and moulded to fit modern preconceptions.

which this accumulating understanding progresses. And also, with social studies, the commonest fault is to think in terms of content; beginning with simple scientific processes at work in the home and in things familiar. It is not solely bits of knowledge that accumulate in the child's understanding, but also the *process* of scientific understanding. Thought must also be given to the stages by which that process is best developed. It certainly is not something inherent in or self-evident to children. In general, it seems reasonable to represent it as following the scheme outlined earlier: starting at the mythic stage by developing a general opposition between what is science and what is not science; exploring during the romantic stage the limits and the bizarre aspects, to better define what science is; classifying and organizing the domain of science in terms of very general schemes and theories during the philosophic stage; and the ironic stage represents the achievement of a mature scientific understanding.

## Mythic

At this stage materials should be selected and organized drawing on the principles outlined in chapter 1. Most prominently for science, one will select those things that are most vivid and dramatic which also show key elements of science in opposition to non-science. That is, at the mythic stage, one will provide a general characterization of the domain of science and work to develop the most general concepts on which a later sophisticated scientific understanding may be built. Stories of the dramatic victories of reason over superstition, of observation over received dogma, of science over ignorance or untutored intuition, should be central to the earliest stage of science instruction. Such things as the image of teams of horses failing to pull apart two iron spheres within which there is a vacuum; the early primitive "taming" of fire; the first men challenged by open water, and discovery of the technology of the boat; attempts to fly like birds, and the invention of the airplane; evolution and the forms of life; the wheel and what it made possible; and so on. Systematic instruction in the full details of the principles underlying each of those discoveries is unimportant at this stage. The aim is to establish the very broadest principles about the nature of the world, how it works and how people have discovered how it works and have invented things that cohere with these general principles to better achieve human purposes, and create new purposes.

The kinds of skills required at this stage seem to me to be efficiently developed by means of board games, puzzles, and such like. If children play these at home many of the basic skills of deduction, hypothesis formation and testing, observation, and evidence marshaling, can be presupposed. If children lack the opportunity to play such games frequently at home, then it seem appropriate that schools should provide the opportunity for them. They hardly need to be in formal science—teaching time—but this can be justified for those games that do also convey scientific knowledge appropriate for this stage.

Most of the knowledge to be conveyed at this stage can be organized according to the principles outlined in chapter 1. It should be borne in mind that the story form or game form is only a more formalized version of the central features of any inquiry or discovery technique. A good inquiry or discovery session will provide a limitation of the world to be dealt with, a set of rules, a beginning that sets up an expectation, a middle that elaborates it and investigates it, and an end that satisfies the original expectation.

## Romantic

The capacities of the romantic stage are best developed and engaged by knowledge of the extreme and the bizarre, which serve better to define for students the boundaries of science. It is at this stage that students will be most interested in magic, superstitions, the byways of science, like alchemy, and so on. This interest is not one to suppress, because it is the means by which students will develop a clearer sense of the limits of science and of its uses and values. To suppress rather than to teach about these things is simply to deprive students of a means of clarifying just what science is. Teaching about magic and alchemy, and what people have hoped to achieve by use of these methods, obviously does not entail propagating them. Rather, it is a means of showing that science is constructed from methods of investigation like alchemy, but it has been refined to include only those things that work—discarding those things that do not work. The crucial romantic development in understanding science involves this image of it as a dynamic form of inquiry, rather than a static set of rules. It is dynamic in that it is nothing more or less than those things that have been found to work—anything that works is incorporated into it. At any stage, science is just those methods that have proved to work best for finding things out and doing things.

Access to scientific knowledge at the romantic stage may best come through the lives of scientists, seeing the knowledge they create, not so much as pieces accumulating, but rather as the expression of human energy, courage, and genius. If a major purpose of science teaching is to initiate students into the habits and methods of scientific inquiry and knowledge securing, then at the romantic stage it is important to introduce them to, and help them associate with, the transcendent human qualities that make scientific discipline possible. There is nothing to emulate, and little to be stirred by, in an inert body of knowledge; there is much to emulate and be stirred by seeing human energy and courage expended in securing that knowledge. By this means the knowledge, however abstruse, can be made humanly meaningful to students at this stage.

It is, then, the great figures and dramatic events that will best serve the development of the capacities of this stage; Galileo and his struggles; Newton and his apple; Einstein and his humility; from Mendel to the structure of DNA. The great story and its great figures looking for what works will give a sense of the remarkable adventure we have been launched on.

In addition, at the romantic stage, students should be encouraged to investigate *something* in minutest detail—whether spiders' webs, the technology of bridges, the reproduction of flowers, or whatever.

## Philosophic

By this stage students have developed a sense of the domain of science, and their interest shifts to mapping that domain, to understanding the general laws of the sciences, to a concern with philosophy of science, with methodology and the process of scientific progress. They are interested primarily in those things that promise general truths about their place and role in things; in the structure of matter and the universe, the nature of life, of existence, of the mind, and so on. Their focus of interest is meta-physics, meta-biology, meta-chemistry, cosmology. Their interest in more particular details is determined by how far such knowledge seems to them likely to clarify the general laws or metaphysical principles in which they locate the most important truths.

## Ironic

Entailed in the development of the capacities of the ironic stage is a mythic sense of the drama of science, a romantic sense of exploring its limits, a philosophic urge for general meaning and significance, all controlled by an ironic appreciation for the overriding importance of the particular, of what can be observed and measured, and of what works. This stage represents a mature, flexible, scientific under-standing.

It is appropriate to repeat here a point I have labored above. I argued that the mature historical understanding does not come from rushing students to an advanced academic method of work, skimping or suppressing the capacities properly developed during the romantic and philosophic stages, contrary to what many teachers and aca-demics seem to believe. Such a procedure seems to produce only impoverished historiographical pedantry. Similarly, with science, moving rapidly to mature forms of scientific investigation—and this can be done while dealing with apparently simple topics like "science around the home" and skimping or repressing romantic and philo-sophic interests—will likely produce only impoverished scientific pedantry. Romantic and philosophic interests in science are often resisted because they seem focused on immature sensationalism or wild-eyed generalizing, but when these impulses are controlled by a developed ironic intelligence they are important constituents of a mature and flexible scientific understanding.

## MATHEMATICS

This theory is concerned primarily with meaning, and it focuses on how one may best make things meaningful to children and students at the various stages of their development. It is clear at present that mathematics as a kind of language remains largely meaningless to most students. They progress no further than the crudest level of computation, which is, we are told, only a part of the prerequisite for grasping something of what mathematics is about.

I noted earlier that educational development involves a dialectical interaction between intellectual or psychological development and a logical sequencing of some discipline areas. Student teachers are usually offered characterizations of psychological development and also a logical sequence in which the knowledge of their particular curriculum area may be organized. The relationship between the two is rarely dealt with and is almost never characterized systematically. This schizophrenia—this lack of connection between mind and curriculum content—seems nowhere more pronounced than in mathematics.

The relationship between the child's and the student's typical conceptual development and the kinds of mathematical knowledge that best supports and is appropriate to the particular stages of that development is a little-discussed topic. Piaget approaches the subject, but his concern is less with mathematics than the psychological development of the child. His reports of experiments do not go on to discuss the appropriate mathematics curriculum that is best supported by the conceptual developments he elucidates with genius. He has made no systematic attempt to relate his psychological findings to mathematics in order to produce an educational theory that might guide teachers. And no one else seems to have done this either.

The question is, how does one organize mathematics so that it best supports and coheres with children's intellectual development to lead most efficiently to the most sophisticated mathematical understanding? It seems that the numerate few have little idea about how to organize their knowledge to make it meaningful to the young.

What engagement with mathematics is meaningful at the mythic level? A pleasure in discovery of what works, how computations may be built, patterns formed, puzzles solved? And at the romantic level? A search for the limits of mathematics and logic in wrestling with Zeno's paradoxes, Russell's paradox, Lewis Carroll's play with basic logical notion, and the kinds of games—though probably at a simpler level—that Martin Gardner's Dr. Matrix sets for readers of the *Scientific American*? And at the philosophic level? A focus toward how mathematics and logic work, its laws and principles, and the firmness of its foundations and their source? And at the ironic level? The most sophisticated present uses of mathematics, whatever they may be.

## COUNSELING

These stages at their most general say something about how children and students make sense of the world and their experience, and as such seem to have in them something of interest to the counselor's role. We give meaning to our lives by plotting the events we experience into patterns—we make stories of them. These plots or stories determine how we feel about the events of our lives, and, on the basis of our feelings, we make decisions about what we should do. At different stages, the *kinds* of stories into which we plot our lives differ and the bases on which we make decisions differ.

Lawrence Kohlberg has already pointed out the folly of discussing moral issues with a young child while using reasoning that presupposes a maturity the child lacks. The result is more or less meaninglessness to the child. Similarly, if the world and choices are presented in terms appropriate to stages in advance of those to which a child or student has developed, the result will be meaningless. If, for example, a meaningful choice of career requires the development of certain philosophic capacities, then to offer freedom of choice in such a case to someone who has not developed those capacities is simply to offer randomness of choice. Many crucial choices require the development of specific capacities to be meaningful. Freedom cannot exist until the relevant capacities are mastered.

This theory offers to the counselor a set of stages which characterize how people make sense of their experience and derive meaning from the world. They may be useful as supplements to those offered by various psychologists, particularly when matters of educational development are foremost.

If the counselor is to address students in terms appropriate to, i.e., meaningful to, the student's stage of development, then tools for diagnosing what stage the student is at are required. Lacking such diagnostic tools at present, one can only advise the counselor to ask students what they read, what they watch on television, what they like best about these. The answers to such questions should allow fairly adequate general diagnoses.

# CONCLUSIONS

There are a number of issues to be considered in this concluding chapter. One set concerns the nature of the process of educational development and what general characterizations of it this theory leads us toward. A further set considers the status of this theory as it has been sketched above. Just what have we got? What use is it in its present form?

## I

Educational development is a process. We reach an advanced stage only by passing through prior and prerequisite stages. We cannot reach the advanced stage directly. This seems obvious enough, but it is frequently ignored. Many well-meaning teachers see creativity or freedom or disciplined scholarship as ideals of education, and, ignoring the fact that these represent the most sophisticated achievements of the best educated, they try to impose them on children. The teacher's proper concern should be with the prerequisite stages and activities which will lead to these achievements.

Teachers should be mostly concerned with helping people through stages of immaturity, enabling them eventually to achieve maturity. There is nothing wrong or shameful about being immature when young. If one has a distaste for the immature and their various modes of expression and kinds of interests, then there is no point trying to teach. Such teachers will be at constant odds with what the child needs most. If one delights in the expressions and interests of the immature, finding them most congenial, then there is no point trying to teach. Such teachers, who are usually immature themselves, will be concerned to keep children immature and will not help them—even if they could—to achieve greater maturity. We might wisely be equally wary of those who seem ashamed of having been young and those who see childhood as the best life has to offer.

## II

I have tried to describe how the process of educational development naturally unfolds in western cultures given the most supportive environment. It is worth stressing, because it brings out one of the most distinctive features of *educational* development: the appropriate environment is made up primarily of *knowledge*. Focusing on educational development brings knowledge to the forefront because it is the fuel of the process, it is the environment which provides aliments for the process to unfold, it is the reactive agent to the proactive functioning of the appropriate genes. Without knowledge there is no education; with little knowledge there is little education. There may be ignorant happy people, and ignorant psychologically well-adjusted people, and ignorant socially well-integrated people, and ignorant physically strong people, and ignorant good people, but there are no ignorant educated people. If a person is largely ignorant of the world and lacks the conceptual distinctions and categories that only knowledge can provide, that person lacks the means to develop the capacities on whose progressive unfolding educational development depends.

## III

One way of characterizing the general process of educational development is as a gradual escape from the domination of the story form. At the mythic stage, the story form is dominant in children's modes of making sense of things. By the ironic stage, stories in any of the forms discussed above may be entertaining, but they no longer dominate or determine the way the person makes sense of things. I have already discussed this view of educational development as a move from the domination of the mind's formal requirements for sense making, which initially impose a rather simple set of categories and relationships on the world and experience, through the elaboration and sophistication of these categories and relationships, to the (ironic) point where they conform as closely as possible to the particulars of the world and experience.

The decreasing need for firm endings—for the simple story form—is reflected trivially in the decreasing inclination to use the exclamation mark. At the mythic stage, nearly every sentence seems worthy of being concluded with an exclamation mark. At the romantic stage, it is used liberally to stress the wonders of the world. At the philosophic stage, it is reserved for those statements which best conform with the general scheme. At the ironic stage, it is rarely used!

This lessening hold of the story form over the mind is allied to the other general characterization I have touched on above: educational development as a move outward from the self to the world, as a move away from the narcissistic distortions that serve the psychological demands of the ego, to an appreciation of the autonomy and particularity of the world.

In light of these characterizations, another that is suggested by the process sketched in the first four chapters seems to present something of a paradox. Educational development has been characterized in various ways as a process that works from outside limits inward. The mythic stage ignores the restrictions of reality whenever convenient, proliferating impossible creatures and worlds that never existed; the romantic stage works to confine thought within reality while exploring its limits; the philosophic stage charts the general features of reality in more detail; and the ironic stage explores particulars.

This general process seems to be repeated within each stage as well. Entry to a stage involves engaging the most general characteristics of the stage and then gradually refining them. For example, entry to the romantic stage involves engagement with the most extreme and bizarre aspects of reality, with new sentiments largely out of control, with an insecure sense of where the limits of the real are, and then these are gradually brought under greater control. Entry to the philosophic stage involves generating the most crude and general scheme, which is then gradually refined and sophisticated. Entry to the ironic stage, I have not discussed in any detail above, but it too involves a sort of sudden grasp at a new manner of making sense of things that is initially general and vague and is gradually refined. In another context, I have called this initial move to the ironic stage *alienating irony;*[1] the sense of alienation following from letting go of the philosophic general schemes and suddenly finding oneself adrift as it were in a sea of particularity, bereft of the orientation provided by the general scheme. It takes time and courage to establish orientation within the shifting world that is the lot of the ironic mind.

Entry to a stage, then, is not achieved by gradual development and mastery of its characteristics. The foundations of each stage are, indeed, developed during the previous stages, but the actual transitions come more like a sudden vision, a sudden coalescence that creates a qualitatively different way of making sense of things. If we reflect on our own educational development, most people can remember such relatively sudden transitions. They are clearly crucial to educational development, but, like most important educational phenomena, have received very little attention, because they are not brought into focus by non-educational theories of development.

At all stages of development we require intellectual security within a world that is suffused at its heart with mystery. The world

---

[1] Kieran Egan, "Progress in Historiography," *Clio*, fall, 1978.

is made up of infinite particularity and endless transformations. Our minds can handle only relatively few concepts at once and only relatively simple processes. Our intellectual struggle is constantly to reduce the particularity and transformations of the world to categories and processes that, on the one hand, are within our intellectual grasp, and, on the other, do not falsify the particulars or transformations of the world or do too much violence to them. All our laws of physics and generalizations in history are attempts thus to simplify the world without falsifying it.

Entry to each stage of educational development represents a qualitative leap in the kind of simplification that is made of the world. Each leap means letting go of a past, simpler security and immediately setting about the task of achieving a new security by collapsing the world to the newly coalesced mental categories. The initial fit of world to categories will permit only a relatively crude picture. Progress through the stage will be indicated in terms of the elaboration and refinement of the categories, achieved by gradually accommodating to the particularity of the world.

We have a process that may be characterized in one of its dimensions as moving outward from the self and in another dimension as moving inward to the particulars of the world. Can we put these two together, to arrive at an even more general characterization of the process? Surely the more general characterization is the mystical insight discussed in the conclusion to chapter 4: as we forget the self, we get closer to reality. Craziness of one kind or another results from getting lost within the self, confusing mental categories with reality, trying to make the intractible world conform to narcissistic requirements.

If these general characterizations of the process are reasonably accurate, they lead to the many unfashionable curriculum recommendations made throughout the book: the central importance of content; the introduction of much more knowledge about the world and human experience in the early grades; the presentation of very general schemes, ideologies, and metaphysical systems in the late grades and college years; the selection of romantic elements at the expense of causal processes in the early secondary years; and so on.

Given my initial claim that this theory is like no other presently available in education, it would be more surprising if it did not yield some unfashionable recommendations.

## IV

My image of these stages is not one of a simple linear progression. Apart from the complexities touched on in chapter 5, I see the stages as having something of a cyclical quality. That is, the mythic and philosophic stages have some significant features in common, as do the romantic and ironic stages. Both the mythic and philosophic stages involve seeking meaning primarily from the general or paradigmatic, whereas the romantic and ironic stages seek meaning primarily in the particular. Put simplistically, the mythic and philosophic stages seem to exercise primarily deductive thinking; the romantic and ironic stages, inductive.

## V

Something that may be evident from chapter 7, which I should thus confess before being accused of, is that this theory seems to fit the humanities better than the sciences. The comments I have made about learning the sciences at various stages may seem more a matter of hints about motivation rather than the learning of scientific concepts.

## VI

This book presents an original and comprehensive theory of educational development. On what bases does it rest, and what use is it in this form? My claims for this small book are hardly modest. I have argued that education is a largely confused field of study because it relies very heavily on non-educational theories. The extent of my immodesty might begin to shine through as I claim that this book is rare in modern educational literature in that it offers an original and comprehensive *educational* theory. Having exposed excessive immodesty, I must now immediately become excessively defensive. The following discussion of the status of this theory is in part an attempt to respond to some anticipated criticisms. The trouble with this as a defensive procedure, of course, is that in seeming to anticipate a critical onslaught, one may suggest all kinds of objections that might otherwise have remained muted. Still, even at the risk of overdoing it, I think it useful to clarify my frequent assertion that, unlike the non-educational theories currently prominent in education, this theory focuses thinking and research on important educational matters.

What are the main features that will distinguish an educational theory from, say, a learning theory borrowed from psychology and applied in education? Theories are generated to account for a range of phenomena. To be plausible, a learning theory must attempt to account for the phenomena people associate with learning. One important prerequisite for generating a theory is a sense of the limits of the phenomena to be dealt with. The theory may then define or redefine those limits more precisely, sometimes in ways not originally anticipated, and focus attention on particular aspects of the phenomena and away from others. Consider behaviorist and field theories of learning: they were generated to account for the same range of phenomena but provide different definitions of just what phenomena should be considered a part of learning and focus attention on different aspects of the phenomena. Despite these differences, however, the range of agreement about what psychological learning theories have to account for is much greater and more precise than people's sense of the range of phenomena an educational theory must account for. In this case, it is a question of what about development is less relevant to a theory of educational development and what should form the central focus of such a theory.

Psychological theories—of development and of learning—now have available a wealth of data, and, more significant in the present context, a range of theories that attempt to account for those data. These theories, moreover, have had a brief, but intense, history of testing, comparison, and refinement, to the point where a newcomer may approach the appropriate phenomena with the help of a variety of well-defined distinctions, categories, characterizations, and the other guides and organizers comprehensive theories provide. Despite disagreements, psychologists may feel a degree of security in dealing with their phenomena of interest that is still unknown to educators.

The above is to make the simple point that education as a field of study is in a more primitive stage of scientific development than even quite insecure fields like psychology and sociology. Education is still, to use Thomas S. Kuhn's term, "pre-paradigmatic."[2] Consequently a comprehensive educational theory at this stage of the game *cannot* look like a comprehensive theory developed within methodologically more advanced fields of study. A truly educational theory will of necessity look unfamiliar at this point because education is largely a theory-free field.

This theory does not come with the kind of detailed empirical support one would expect of, say, a new learning theory.[3] We do not have years of educational-theory guided research to provide a set of tested categories, distinctions, characterizations, and a body of data secured in the process of testing previous theories. A new learning theory at this stage does have such a set of categories, distinctions, characterizations, and data to draw on. In education, we still require very general theories to organize and define the appropriate range of phenomena.

Having articulated what I claim is such a theory, why have I not engaged in the empirical research whose (presumed) support would have enabled me to put it forward with greater security? Had I but

[2] See Thomas S. Kuhn, *The Structure of Scientific Revolutions* (Chicago: University of Chicago Press, 1962).

[3] Many people in education assume that a theory about learning is necessarily an educational theory. It is this kind of assumption that has caused such confusion in education. Typical psychological theories of learning are as little related to education as typical psychological theories of development. We simply do not have an educational theory of learning. Such a theory would focus, not on the mechanics of the learning process, but on those aspects of learning of most importance to education. It would be a theory that does not separate learning from motivation, and that would distinguish at least gross categories something like "inert," "aliment," and "entertaining" learning, and it would have a lot to say about kinds of knowledge. I will elaborate this point in the following section.

world enough and time, it would no doubt have been desirable to have gone about it that way. But even if I had the research skills, it would take a single person an inordinate amount of time to develop adequate empirical support for the full range of claims made by this theory. Ideas must precede data; what I am doing here is offering some ideas that might help us to get at data of educational significance. And the principle of division of labor must operate here.

The range of claims open to empirical testing runs from the particular to the very general. The more general and significant the claim, the more time, resources, and ingenuity will have to be expended in testing it. For this reason, we might expect to see more particular claims tested first, and, should they prove the theory more or less correct, tests of more general claims will likely be considered worthwhile. There are very general claims about the process of education, quite general claims about the division of the process into stages, and relatively particular claims about the characteristics of each stage. It may be worth while just to sketch roughly some of the areas that seem empirically falsifiable.

One might begin with tests of the accuracy and adequacy of what are claimed to be the defining characteristics of each stage. For example, with children who may be assumed to be at the mythic stage, one might test whether material organized according to the principles outlined above is in fact more meaningful—better understood and remembered—than the same material organized in various other forms. A similar kind of test could be run at each stage.

To move up a degree of generality, one might test the validity of the stage distinctions. Is the sequence invariable? Can we not find children using relatively sophisticated philosophic organizers without having developed those of the romantic stage? Or, to take a case that at present receives no support from other developmental theories: Is it true that well-educated students go through the kind of change in their focus of interest which this theory calls the move from the romantic to the philosophic stage?

One might take some material carefully organized in a philosophic manner, though in simple language, and have children and students at the mythic, romantic, and philosophic stage study it. I have claimed that such material would be largely meaningless to those at the earlier stages. It would be interesting to see just what kind of meaning those at the earlier stages derive from it, and how those in the three stages understood the material differently. It would be interesting to see whether significant differences correlated more highly with my stages than with something else, such as, for example, IQ.

The above presuppose, of course, that one can diagnose fairly well what stage a student is in. At present, it should be possible to make a preliminary diagnosis with sufficient accuracy for the above tests by analysis of individual children's interests, writing, reading.

Should the more particular tests support the theory—though no doubt forcing revisions and refinements in the process—one might organize a longitudinal study of relatively large numbers of students from diverse backgrounds. They should be taught from kindergarten to postgraduate years (or to school-leaving age) by principles as close as possible to those given above. At maturity, we would expect to find those students significantly higher than the national average on all measures of educational achievement. No doubt Hawthorne effect and irrelevant improvements in instruction caused by forcing careful organization of teaching would interfere with the clarity of the results, but, if the theory is largely accurate, the degree of educational superiority of the experimental group should be sufficiently dramatic to rule out these as primary causes. An analytic rather than experimental test might be run by seeing how far the characteristics of the ironic stage are evident in the works of those recognized as the most outstanding scholars.

A clearer distinction between a psychological and educational theory can be identified. Any developmental theory should indicate an end toward which the process develops, and being explicit about this end should involve some image of what is desirable as a product of the process. Psychological theories tend to be somewhat coy when it comes to characterizing the desirable end products or end states of the processes they identify, referring occasionally to statistical norms or some notion of what is natural, but more frequently leaving the end product as an implicit and largely unexamined assumption. An educational theory must be more explicit about the desirable end product, and, consequently, it will have as a central component normative claims. That is, it will involve a concept of an ideally, or desirably, educated person. Testing the appropriateness or desirability of this normative component in an educational theory is essentially a philosophical matter. One might argue that some philosophical sophistication is a necessary prerequisite to being able to deal sensibly with an educational theory—to a degree that is not true in fields whose theories lack such a centrally placed normative element.

A further clear distinction between educational and psychological theories has been touched on in the second conclusions section above. Prominent in educational theories will be a concern with knowledge, or content, whereas this may be entirely absent or incidental in psychological theories. A psychological theory of learning, for example, may properly have nothing to say about *what* is learned or its value, but an educational theory will dwell extensively on what should be learned and will be concerned with the relative values of different kinds of content.

If articulating an original and comprehensive theory in a largely theory-free field presents a challenge to the writer, judging its adequacy presents a not altogether dissimilar intellectual challenge to the reader. Our typical response to a new theory claiming educational significance or implications is to judge it in light of the determining paradigm operating in the field and to view it in the context of other theories dealing with the same phenomena, comparing its explanatory power, the economy whereby it organizes the data, and so on, with their's. In this case, we lack such means of comparison and such a helpful paradigm, and I have argued the inappropriateness of judging it on grounds we would apply to non-educational theories. How, then, are we to judge the theory's adequacy? What are its bases?

Initially, we must judge by how well answers are produced for questions like the following. How adequately does the theory make sense of the phenomena it purports to deal with? How sensibly does it identify and define what phenomena should form the focus of a theory of educational development? How well do its categories, distinctions, and characterizations cohere with our own observation and experience? How well do these categories help us think more fruitfully about educational development? How accurately does the theory embody all the relevant data? Are there some data which cannot be accommodated to this theory? How well does the theory focus on the things we intuitively consider centrally important to educational development? Does it generate new claims, the testing of which will create knowledge of educational significance?

That is to say, for the initial judgement of the adequacy of this theory readers are thrown back on common sense, reflection on their own observations and experience, and inference from their knowledge about educational development. To claim, for example, because Piaget interprets the obsessive collecting activities of students (in what I call the romantic stage) as learning about hierarchies of classes and seriation and I interpret it as an exploration of the extent and limits of reality, that my interpretation is wrong or in need of defence against Piaget's interpretation is an inappropriate way of judging the adequacy of my theory. The two interpretations are, of course, not incompatible—they focus on a different degree of generality and refer to different aspects of the development process. Piaget is concerned with particular conceptual developments. My focus is on more general educational developments. Piaget's interpretation is coherent with my general characterization of the process of development through the romantic stage; the development of increasingly abstract concepts is integral to the development of hierarchies of classes and seriation. An original educational theory must be judged initially by application of the tools of common sense, because education as it presently stands offers no further technical help.

In a largely theory-free field, a new theory cannot be generated from refinement or revision or expansion of current theories, as is common in more scientifically advanced fields of study. One may, of course, draw something useful from other theories that touch on similar phenomena, or on the same phenomena from different per-

spectives. But the theory must derive primarily from close familiarity with the phenomena being dealt with and constant observation
of its processes. One then categorizes the results of one's observation,
using conceptual tools from any source at all that offers something
helpful. For example, my four major categories owe something to
anthropology, poetics, and philosophy of history. One tests the
categories by constantly referring them back to the phenomena and
one elaborates them by absorbing any relevant data that may be
gleaned from any source. The bases of this theory are observation
and reflection, a study of research findings about development, and
a touch of speculation. It is these, too, that the reader must bring to
evaluating the theory.


# VII

Psychology attempts to isolate certain phenomena and generate
theories that explain them. So we have distinct psychological theories of development, of learning, of motivation, and so on. It seems
to be commonly assumed that education too will generate distinct
educational theories of development, learning, motivation, and so
on. But the educator's interest in, say, motivation, is significantly
different from that of the psychologist. For the educator, the problem of motivation can better be expressed as a concern with how we
interest students in learning specific things we consider valuable.
The *things* is important to educators—we are less interested in
isolating and explaining a phenomenon called motivation than in
understanding how we can engage students' interest in certain
things. That is, we are concerned with an interactive phenomenon.
We might sensibly conclude that talk of motivation in education is a
red herring; it does not help to better formulate the education
question of how we may best engage interest in particular things,
and it tends to direct our attention away from the interactive process
which should properly be our concern.

A similar point can be made about learning. Education is not
concerned with isolating a phenomenon called learning and gener-

ating theories about it, so much as with the question of how we can best ensure that students learn specific things of value. Again, our proper focus of concern is an interactive phenomenon.

In addition, we should note that knowing how to engage students' interests in specific things of value is much the same—given the level of generality of education's concerns—as knowing how best to help students learn specific things of value. That is, for education, motivation, or engaging interest, and learning are inextricably interconnected. Further, we know that students' interest in, and their ability to learn, specific things change during the course of their development. Given education's level of concern, we may say that motivation, learning, and development, from an educational point of view, are not really distinct phenomena. Trying to characterize, say, the changes during the process of development in some more or less systematic way, as I have done above, is to generate a theory that is concerned with motivation and learning, as well as development.

This might seem like a megalomaniacal attempt to claim to have conquered a continent while having barely a toe-hold on the beach, but it is rather a suggestion of how educational theory and research can be, and have been, misled by drawing so heavily and uncritically from psychology. My conclusion is not that I am sketching theories of learning, motivation, *and* development, but rather that the focal phenomena of education are more uniform and coherent than appears to be the case if one views education as an architectonic discipline which should draw its theories from outside disciplines. The primary concern of education is how to teach the young certain things of value in a manner which will ensure that those things will be engaging, meaningful, and most clearly understood by the young during the various periods of their educational development. Which is to claim that education will admit only theories of education, not distinct theories of learning, motivation, development, and so on. A proper theory of education will entail claims, some of them normative, about learning, motivation, and development, and it will yield direct implications for curriculum, policy, classroom structure. But none of these things can be sensibly dealt with from an educational point of view apart from a theory of education. That is, discussions of policy, or of design of classrooms, etc., require for sensible resolution a theory of education to direct them. I can now revise my claim for this book and say that what it offers is not a theory of development, but a theory of education.

## VIII

Sections of this book may read like a polemic against non-educational theories of development, learning, motivation. Of course, I do not intend this. The polemical notes in this book are aimed at the uncritical use, or abuse, of these theories in education. Having said this, however, I want to make a point that will already be obvious to those readers familiar with non-educational theories of development; that is, that I am enormously indebted to non-educational theories of development and the data they have generated. In particular, the influence of Piaget's and Erikson's works will be everywhere evident to those familiar with them. Less evident, and less expectedly perhaps, is my great debt to the work of Northrop Frye.[4] This theory of education has drawn heavily and eclectically from such work.

I have argued that the main cause of the ineffectualness of much educational research is that it has been working with borrowed, non-educational theories, under paradigms that direct attention away from educational issues. As I have already indicated in the previous section, one use of this theory in its present form is that testing it will direct empirical research to focus on issues of educational significance.

To end, I can do no better than quote Plato's comment on his educational theory: "Heaven knows whether it is true; but this, at any rate, is how it appears to me."[5]

---

[4] Especially his *Anatomy of Criticism* (Princeton: Princeton University Press, 1957).
[5] Plato *Republic* 7. 517 (trans. Francis MacDonald Cornford, New York: Oxford University Press, 1945), p. 231.

# INDEX

LB1570 .E384          CU-Main

Egan, Kieran. cn/Educational development / Kieran

3 9371 00003 3936

LB
1570        Egan, Kieran
E384         Educational development

| DATE DUE | | | |
|---|---|---|---|
| MAR 08 '93 | | | |
| | | | |
| | | | |
| | | | |
| | | | |
| | | | |
| | | | |
| | | | |
| | | | |
| | | | |
| | | | |
| | | | |

CONCORDIA COLLEGE LIBRARY
2811 N. E. HOLMAN ST.
PORTLAND, OREGON 97211